Thank God for the Crumbs

Bonnie Kotter

REVIEW AND HERALD PUBLISHING ASSOCIATION

Washington, DC 20039-0555
Hagerstown, MD 21740

Copyright © 1986 by
Review and Herald Publishing Association

This book was
Edited by Gerald Wheeler
Designed by Richard Steadham
Cover photo by David B. Sherwin
Type set: 11/12 Palatino

PRINTED IN U.S.A.

Library of Congress Cataloging in Publication Data

Kotter, Bonnie, 1941-
    Thank God for the crumbs.

    1. Christian life—Seventh-day Adventist authors.
I. Title.
BV4501.2.K68   1986   286.7'32'0922   [B]   85-24461

ISBN 0-8280-0315-7

CONTENTS

1
Thank God for the Crumbs

Newly married Yvonne Stemple had just arrived home from her first day back at her secretarial job following a storybook wedding and honeymoon. Her minister husband, Jeff, wasn't home.

In two weeks they would be conducting their first evangelistic series as a married couple, and tonight they were to begin visiting some interested families. Their first appointment was for seven o'clock.

No time to lose—we must be on the road in an hour, Yvonne thought as she hurriedly entered her picture-perfect kitchen to prepare supper. As she stepped into it, however, her enthusiasm for cooking suddenly vanished. Before her on the counter—just in front of the mint-green ruffled curtains—stood open jars of peanut butter and jam. The jar of jam dripped strawberry preserves down its sides into a sticky pool at its base. To the right of the jam was an open bag of whole-wheat bread. A trail of crumbs led from the bread bag to the toaster and finally ended at the peanut butter and jam jars.

As she walked to the counter, something crunched beneath her feet. Yvonne squealed and jumped backward. On the floor in front of her lay a toasted crust of bread—and *more crumbs!*

A closer look at the peanut butter and jam jars revealed traces of peanut butter in the strawberry jam, strawberry jam in the peanut butter—and crumbs in both.

Yvonne's neat, organized, everything-in-its-place mind

reeled. During their courtship, Jeff and she had discussed all the weighty issues of life. Theirs was not a love-at-first-sight relationship. Only after working together in spiritual outreach programs did they begin considering each other as more than temporary associates.

While dating, they had thoroughly explored their spiritual and material goals, handling of finances, personal interests—even politics. They had prayed regularly, together and as individuals, for guidance from God as to their possible union. And finally, to ensure that they had overlooked nothing, they participated in counseling sessions with a mutually respected minister. On all the major issues of life they had been in perfect agreement. But never once did they discuss the routine duties of life.

As the weeks went by, it became more and more apparent to Yvonne that she and Jeff had irreconcilable differences in the way they performed everyday chores.

One evening, because of an appointment, Yvonne could not fold the freshly laundered towels, so she asked Jeff, who had a rare evening at home, to do it for her. She had organized the linen closet with hand towels, washcloths, and bath towels neatly folded and stacked according to kind in specific areas. However, when she returned that evening, she found the newly washed towels folded in a different way from those already in the closet and with hand towels, washcloths, and bath towels intermingled in one colossal stack. When she protested that the towels were disorganized, Jeff simply said, "What difference does it make? They're all *clean*, aren't they?"

"That isn't the point. The point is that when all the towels are mixed together you must rummage through the whole stack to find the type of towel you need."

Shrugging, he settled back in his living room easy chair and continued reading *The History of the Reformation of the Sixteenth Century*, by D'Aubigné.

Though such incidents caused irritations, one particular point of contention produced endless debates—Jeff's sermons. He considered his sermons "theological stimulation," while Yvonne considered them "theoretical exercises." After each one, she would carefully dissect it, telling him how he could have rephrased specific statements to make them more practical and applicable to the parishioners. Patiently he listened to her criticism week after week and in an even-tempered tone analyzed what she was saying. Then calmly he would resolve the conversation by saying, "Well, I guess I'll just have to do better."

But as months passed his sermons remained, according to her, "dry" and "above the heads of the people." So troubled was she by them that she began making them a matter of prayer. Each morning, in her private devotions, she pleaded, "Oh, Lord, please help my husband become a good preacher. Help him to become practical in his preaching and make the Bible live for his congregation."

One Friday evening, about ten o'clock, as Yvonne was reading in bed, her husband stood in the doorway of their bedroom. Etched in light from the hallway, his six-foot-two-inch frame monopolized the entrance to the room, yet his sheepish expression made him appear timid and boyish.

"Would you read this through and tell me what you think of it?" he asked as he held out his sermon to Yvonne.

Determined that she was not going to initiate a disagreement about its contents, she smiled and said, "Sure, honey."

Jeff walked toward the bed and handed her the sermon. Then he sat on the edge of the bed, awaiting her verdict.

Yvonne took the sermon from his hand, silently praying that *this* time the sermon would be practical. As she read, however, she could feel herself becoming irritated. The sermon contained poetic language, theoretical concepts, and a smattering of Karl Barth and Paul Tillich (world-renowned theologians).

Finished, she decided to try a different approach. Instead of taking specific sentences and trying to improve on them, she decided to ask questions and try to get him to think through the sermon for himself.

7

"You have some good concepts in here," she said in as optimistic a tone as she could. "But what is this sermon saying to the people? What message do you want them to take home and live out in their lives?"

His jaw tightened. "Well," he said as he slapped his knee and stood to his feet, "I've done the best I could. If you don't like this sermon, *you* can rewrite it. I'm going to bed."

Yvonne had never seen Jeff exasperated before. His silent, strong demeanor had always appeared to her as unflappable. But although she knew she had pushed him too far, her pride and determination to show him that even she, without a seminary education, could do better, responded to his challenge. "OK, I *will* rewrite it."

Scuffing into her slippers, Yvonne put on her robe and headed down the hallway toward Jeff's study as he grabbed his pajamas from a closet hook and disappeared into the bathroom for his bedtime shower.

Ruffled and flushed, she sat down at his typewriter and began reworking his sermon. She took Jeff's concepts and inserted illustrations that applied them to everyday life. The Bible texts that he had carefully researched she related to contemporary experiences. Then she culminated the sermon into a challenge of commitment.

At 1:30 A.M. she had finished her reworked masterpiece. Yvonne sat back in Jeff's desk chair and read it through. Satisfied that the "flock" would be fed *this* week, she went to bed.

Without a word of remonstrance the next morning, Jeff accepted the revised sermon, practiced it before breakfast, and delivered it flawlessly, with all the necessary dynamics, to his congregation at the 11:00 A.M. worship service.

As Yvonne and her husband stood side by side at the back of the sanctuary greeting church members, her heart swelled with pride as she heard several members comment:

"That was a wonderful sermon, Pastor."

"You sure told it like it is."

"I certainly appreciated your message today."

"That sermon spoke right to my heart, Pastor."

The ride home from church, however, was rather quiet. Jeff, who always found it necessary to discuss problems openly, finally brought up the subject of the sermon. "As you know, the members liked the sermon today."

Hearing Jeff make that admission gave Yvonne an inner feeling of triumph. "Now you can see what I've been trying to tell you." As soon as she spoke the words, she knew she had said the wrong thing. Not wanting to make Jeff feel incapable of composing such a sermon, she quickly added, "Now you can do it yourself." The words fell with a silent thud to the floor of the car. She turned toward Jeff to see how he was responding to her comments.

"It's not that easy for me, Yvonne." He kept his eyes straight ahead as he drove, but his wife could see despondency creeping into his gaze. "I can't seem to put the practics in sermons. Even when I try to concentrate on doing so, they don't come out practical."

The admission came from his lips with such labored effort that her triumphant attitude dissolved into concern. As she studied Jeff's face she realized that she had never seen him really troubled before. His firm faith in God, his unfailing courage in the face of obstacles, and his determination to do God's will at all cost were the traits she had so admired in him throughout their courtship. Yvonne had always thought nothing could shake her husband's rock-solid foundation. But now he appeared to be grappling with a situation he wasn't certain he could handle.

What have I done? she thought. Have I brought discouragement to the man I have committed myself to encourage? Ashamed of herself, she switched her tactic to cheerleading. "You can do it, Jeff. All you need to do is read the sermons of some practical preachers and concentrate on their techniques. You can even buy cassettes of good preachers and play them as you drive. Why, we can even visit churches of other denominations that have good preachers and see them in action."

Jeff didn't respond to her forced enthusiasm. It seemed to Yvonne that he had blocked out everything around him to concentrate on his internal struggle.

The rest of the day passed in mechanical visits to hospitalized parishioners. The couple performed the expected duties with politeness, but they seemed separated and distant from each other.

Yvonne awakened before daybreak the next morning. She had not slept well and seemed to remember her husband getting up in the middle of the night. Knowing he was troubled, she felt herself the cause of it.

Marriage is supposed to bring oneness, she thought as she put on her robe and quietly walked to his study. It seems Jeff and I are fighting against each other. I felt more unity with him *before* we were married. We seemed to work more like a team then than now. Could I have made a mistake? Was God really guiding us together? Or did we just think He was because *we* wanted it?

Sitting in his desk chair, she stared out his office window. The first grayness was just beginning to break the darkness of the night, and Venus still blazed through the limbs of the big maple tree outside the second-story window.

"Lord, what is happening to us? Our courtship felt so right. Why does our marriage seem so wrong? We seem so different from each other. Jeff is so much more theoretical than I thought he was. And I feel like I'm turning into a nag trying to change him. I think we really contributed to Your work while we were dating. Now we seem mismatched. When I see the 'sheep' of our church going away spiritually hungry every week, I feel bad. I feel a responsibility to tell my husband what I see and feel, and yet when I say something to him I feel it's the wrong thing. I don't know what to do, God. I feel guilty when I don't say anything and guilty when I do. My deepest desire is to see Jeff become a good preacher, but how can I help him? I'm frustrated, Lord. Obviously my approach this weekend was the wrong one. I proved my point, but I sure learned another meaning to the old saying 'To the victor go the spoils.' "

Quietly Yvonne sat watching a rose-colored streak across the horizon turn to amber. Slowly Venus began to fade in brilliance as blue clouds etched with yellow appeared.

"Who called Jeff to the ministry?" A voice, almost audible, flashed through her mind. As the words penetrated the density of her gloom, she responded, "Why, You did, Lord."

"Then why don't you let *Me* make him a preacher?"

Yvonne stared at the sunrise with bewilderment and wonder. Why, of course, she thought, that's the answer. I've been trying to do the work that God must do in my husband's life. God wants him to be a good preacher far more than I do, and God loves His 'sheep' more than I do too. He knows their needs . . . and He knows Jeff's needs . . . What was it our minister told us during premarital counseling? . . . Oh, yes . . .

"The hardest thing you will have to do in marriage is to accept each other just the way you are. Changing human beings is God's job. Always remember, different isn't wrong."

"Different isn't wrong." The words reverberated through her mind. It's more than just Jeff's preaching, she thought. That's a major issue, but beyond that is the fact that Jeff does things *different* from the way I do them, and I'm trying to remake him.

"Different isn't wrong." Those words didn't mean much before we were married, Yvonne thought, but oh, how I realize their wisdom now. My attempts to remake my husband are separating us from the oneness God wishes us to experience.

As the first shafts of sun rays peeked over the horizon Yvonne slipped to her knees. "Lord, thank You for my husband—just as he is. Help me to be an encouragement to him as I promised to be in our personally written marriage vows. Forgive me for trying to force him into the mold I think right for him. Help me to let go of my desire for my husband in favor of Your desire for him. I commit my husband to You today. You take him and You make him into what You want him to be. With Your help, Lord, from today on I'm going to be only an encouragement to him and love him just as he is. Help me to concentrate on all the wonderful qualities he has that caused me to fall in love with him. And when he preaches, help me to comment only on what I *like* about his sermons."

Yvonne kept her promise to the Lord for the next two weeks. Each time Jeff did something "different" from the way she would have done it, instead of complaining about it, she thanked God for the irritation and asked God to show her what it was in her own life He wished to teach her from it. In the days that followed she began realizing that she was too meticulous, too perfectionistic, too concerned with things being done in a manner she considered to be *right*. And true to her promise, after each sermon she pointed out only the statements or portions of Jeff's presentation she liked. She even wrote them on the back of her church bulletin so she wouldn't forget them.

His preaching didn't improve in those two weeks, but their unity did. On the third weekend they visited her parents, who lived in another State. That same weekend an older and more seasoned minister whom Jeff knew and respected was guest speaker at Yvonne's childhood church. After the worship service, Jeff lingered to chat with Pastor Gordon. During the course of their conversation, the subject turned to preaching.

"I need some work on my sermons," Jeff confided to the visiting minister. "You present such interesting, practical ones. How do you keep on the cutting edge?"

"I read all the sermons I can lay my hands on that notable preachers of the past have given. I'm also a member of a tape-of-the-month club for preachers. And I listen to cassettes as I drive in my car. Another thing I do, Jeff, is go to hear other good preachers—regardless of their denomination. If I hear that someone can preach, I go to listen and study that person's techniques. We as Seventh-day Adventists have a marvelous opportunity to do that since we preach on Saturday morning instead of Sunday."

Yvonne, standing beside her husband, could hardly believe her ears. Those are the very things I told Jeff, she thought to herself. What surprised her was that Jeff was receptive to all Pastor Gordon was saying. He listened as if they were totally new ideas he had never heard before.

Silently Yvonne prayed. "You are so good, Lord. You sent someone whose opinion Jeff respected to say the very things that he couldn't accept hearing from me. Thank You, Lord."

On the way home Jeff commented to Yvonne, "Those were great suggestions Pastor Gordon made for improving my sermons." Then addressing Yvonne's parents, he said, "Mom and Dad, do you know of a good preacher around here that we could go to listen to tomorrow morning?"

They did know of one—Pastor Bertram, a Baptist minister at a local university church who, according to them, "receives raves from all who hear him."

On Sunday morning Jeff and Yvonne attended Pastor Bertram's church. His text for the day was Matthew 5:13. In his sermon he repeatedly stated, "Ye are the salt of the earth." The sermon was so gripping, so powerful, so moving that both Jeff and Yvonne were teary-eyed at its conclusion.

Feeling slightly self-conscious in an unfamiliar church, the couple had sat in the last row at the rear of the sanctuary. Consequently, they were the first to leave, and the first to shake Pastor Bertram's hand as they left.

Still in the wake of his sermon, and undoubtedly moved by the Holy Spirit, Bertram looked Jeff straight in the eye and said, "God wants *you* to be the salt of the earth."

The words hit Jeff with such forcefulness that he stepped back from the minister and stared at him for a moment. Then, awkwardly, he regained his composure, shook the minister's hand, and thanked him for his message of the morning.

Jeff's voice quivered slightly as he and his wife walked down the church steps. "God spoke to me today, Yvonne.

That was great preaching!"

Overcome by the spirit of the service, the power of the message, and the unexpected comment from the Baptist minister, she could not speak for the lump in her throat. All she could manage was a silent prayer to heaven. "Thank You, God. When You want something done, You sure know how to do it. Thank You for helping me get out of Your way."

In the weeks to come, Jeff submerged himself in reading and listening to great sermons. Soon his congregants became ignited with the power of his preaching, and within eight months the church had to add extra chairs to the sanctuary to accommodate the increasing number of people attending the worship services.

It's been nearly twenty years since Yvonne and Jeff first pledged their love to each other. Though the individuality of their personalities have smoothed some of the rough spots in each of them, Yvonne still occasionally finds crumbs on the kitchen sink and in the peanut butter and jam jars. The difference is that she has learned to thank God for the crumbs.

2

Thank God for No Father

It was July, 1971, in north-eastern Illinois, and miniskirts were the fashion.

Genny Anderson sat in the last pew of the filled sanctuary, delighted by the number of community parents attending the Vacation Bible School graduation.

Frilly-dressed little girls and scrubbed-to-a-shine little boys awkwardly climbed the three stairs to the platform at the front of the church to prepare for the kindergarten presentation. The leader and her assistants shuffled the children into order as they reached the platform.

As the line of little people came to its end, Genny noticed Rosie Gonzalez, a teenager about 15 years of age, guiding the rear of the entourage to the steps of the platform. Rosie, a Hispanic beauty of medium height and just slightly overweight, wore a thigh-high miniskirt.

As she positioned herself at the front of the church beneath the platform, one little girl, who had failed to find the steps, darted in front of her. Rosie picked up the little one, turned her back to the audience, and bent over the three steps to place the girl on top of the platform.

The woman seated beside Genny gasped audibly. Genny felt her own cheeks flush. Though keenly mindful of the impression her church was making on the many guests present, Genny's primary thoughts were on behalf of Rosie. Silently she prayed that no one would make a rude comment to the girl about her inappropriate skirt length, or her "indecent exposure."

Genny and her husband had recently moved to Illinois from La Porte, Indiana. Finding no Pathfinder Club at their new church, Genny had volunteered to begin one. Since she enjoyed working with children, she put her whole-hearted effort into making the club a success.

Though sensing that Rosie would never consent to joining something as "immature" as a Pathfinder Club, Genny had a desire to get close to her. The girl radiated a paradox of independent loneliness and ignited a desire in Genny to reach out to her. But the initial efforts had proved unfruitful. Rosie had a sophisticated air about her that at times could be intimidating, and Mrs. Anderson had experienced some of her quick-witted responses. All that she knew about Rosie was that the girl lived alone with her widowed great-aunt, was an excellent student, and displayed strong leadership abilities.

The remainder of the Vacation Bible School program went well, and during the refreshment period that followed, the guests were quite liberal with gracious comments. Genny observed that Rosie was smiling as she left the church that evening, and breathed a prayer of thanks.

Sabbath morning arrived complete with blue sky, a breeze, and low humidity—a welcomed relief from the heat wave they had been having. A perfect day to get a positive response from Rosie, Genny thought as she and her husband drove to Sabbath school.

Upon arriving at the church, she saw Rosie and her great-aunt, Mrs. Garcia, enter the rear door of the church. Mrs. Garcia was always one of the first members to arrive on Sabbath morning. Having had ten children of her own, now all grown, she rejuvenated herself for the week by assisting in the cradle roll Sabbath school. Though her chunky body barely had a lap when it sat down, she still managed to fit one child on each of her knees during Sabbath school and usually during most of the church service.

Entering the church, Genny went immediately downstairs to the cradle roll classroom. Rosie, clad in another thigh-high miniskirt, had just set down some materials that she had helped her great-aunt bring for the morning's class, and was leaving the room as Genny entered.

"Good morning, Rosie."

A reserved response of "Good morning, Mrs. Anderson," a glance at Genny, and the girl continued toward the door.

Quickly Genny turned and began walking alongside her. "Rosie, I came down here to talk to you. Do you have a minute?"

"I guess so," she replied, looking quizzically at the woman.

The two stopped and faced each other.

"Rosie, I need some help, and was wondering if you might consider giving me a hand."

A faint smile and a hint of interest came to Rosie's eyes as she asked, "What kind of help?"

"Well, Rosie, I've had a hard time trying to find assistants to help me with the Pathfinder Club, and I was wondering if you might consent to being one of them. I would need you each Sunday morning from 9:00 A.M. till noon, and since you live along the route I take to church, I could pick you up and take you home. Would you consider it?"

"I might. What would I have to do?"

"Help me maintain order, for one thing," Genny laughed.

Rosie grinned broadly, and Genny knew she had finally pierced the barrier around the teenager.

"I would need you to assist the Pathfinders with the projects they're working on, and of course, I need some good suggestions and ideas for future projects. You know, this is my first crack at Pathfinders. Since I didn't grow up an Adventist, I was never a Pathfinder as a child, and I'm really trailblazing as I go along. I sure need someone that would be willing to trailblaze with me. Are you game?"

By now Genny could see the girl was fully at ease.

"I'm game, if it's all right with my aunt."

"Let's ask her," Genny suggested.

Mrs. Garcia seemed pleased with the arrangement, and the next morning at 8:45 A.M. Genny and Rosie were setting up for Pathfinder Club together.

In the weeks that followed the two grew to be close friends, and Mrs. Anderson became Genny to Rosie. On their rides to and from Pathfinder meetings Rosie began to talk to her about casual topics. Sometimes they would sit in Genny's car outside the girl's home for thirty to forty-five minutes before Rosie would finally go inside.

Soon Genny learned that Rosie's mother lived in Chicago and came to see her daughter once or twice a month. According to Rosie, her mother worked as an interior designer in Chicago because the wages were higher there. Yet Mrs. Gonzalez wanted her daughter to have a Christian education and be raised in a rural setting. So she had arranged for Rosie to live with her great-aunt, the sister of Mrs. Gonzalez's mother, who lived in the country near an Adventist academy. Rosie manifested a deep love for her mother, but never mentioned her father.

One Friday evening as Genny drove Rosie home from a special Pathfinder event, the teenager seemed more talkative than ever.

Mrs. Anderson stopped the car in front of Rosie's home, and Rosie began talking about Kathy, a young person the same age as her, who attended the same church and academy. Rosie began criticizing her for "putting on a show for church members" by saying and doing all the things that church members would want her to in their presence. At the academy, Rosie explained, Kathy said and did things in front of other students that were contrary to the impression she made at church.

Genny listened without making any comment. It appeared to her that Rosie resented the popularity that Kathy enjoyed with the adults at church.

Quite abruptly Rosie concluded her discourse on Kathy, paused for a moment, and then looked straight at Genny as she said, "I know I shouldn't wear miniskirts to church."

Surprised but delighted by the sudden interjection, Mrs. Anderson strove to maintain a calm, nonchalant attitude, and prayed silently for wisdom to know how to handle it.

"I don't wear them to school," Rosie continued.

"Why not?"

"They're not allowed at school, and I shouldn't be wearing them to church, either."

"Then why do you?"

"I love to shake up the adults at church."

Silent for a moment, Genny then asked, "Do I hear you saying that you don't believe it's right to be wearing miniskirts to church?"

"That's right," the girl answered without hesitation.

"And you wear miniskirts to church but not to school?"

"Rrrright." She tipped her head in a cocky fashion and pointed her right index finger toward Mrs. Anderson.

Genny paused for a moment, then said slowly, her voice calm and even, "Rosie, what's the difference between Kathy's attitude and yours?"

The teenage girl's eyes narrowed slightly and her brow furrowed as she pursed her lips and drew them to one side. "H'mmmmm," she murmured, then looked at Genny and nodded her head. "I see what you're getting at. I'm being as hypocritical as Kathy, aren't I?"

Mrs. Anderson said nothing. Inwardly, however, she was thrilled with the awakening she was witnessing in Rosie.

"I'm doing something else I shouldn't be doing either," the girl said a moment later.

"What's that?"

"I'm sneaking out my window at night to go motorcycle riding with a 28-year-old man."

Fighting to maintain self-control, Genny inquired, "Doesn't your aunt suspect anything?"

"No. I just say Good night, tell her I'm going to do some studying, and then go to my room. My grades are good, so why should she suspect?"

Knowing a little about psychology and how often girls raised without fathers seek a father figure in their dating patterns, Genny decided to take a plunge into the girl's life. "Rosie, whatever happened to your father?"

The porch light from Mrs. Garcia's home sent a diffused glow into the car, and Genny could see Rosie's dark eyes glare as she blurted, "I hate him! He deserted my mother when I was just 2 years old. And when I was 6 he sent me a birthday card with my name spelled Rosy. He didn't even know how to spell my name!"

Genny listened to a torrent of bitterness. When the fury abated, she asked, "Does your mother feel resentment toward him too?"

More subdued now, but shaken, Rosie said, "She never talks about him."

After the girl had gained more composure, Mrs. Anderson turned to her and said, "Did you ever think of thanking God for not having a father while you were growing up?"

"Thanking God?" Her eyes grew wide and bewildered. "Are you crazy?"

Genny reached for the Bible that she kept in the glove compartment of her car, turned on the overhead light, and opened the Bible to Ephesians 5:20. "This may sound strange, Rosie, but listen: 'Always give thanks for everything to our God and Father in the name of our Lord Jesus Christ' [T.L.B.]. You'll notice it doesn't say, 'Give thanks for only the *good* things that happen to you.' It says to give thanks for 'everything.'

"You see, Rosie, you are important to God. Let me turn to a text that you may never have heard before. It's found in Psalm 139:14 to 16: 'Thank you for making me so wonderfully complex! It is amazing to think about. Your workmanship is marvelous—and how well I know it. You were there while I was being formed in utter seclusion! You saw me before I was born and scheduled each day of my life before I began to breathe. Every day was recorded in your

Book!' [T.L.B.].

"Rosie, if God 'scheduled each day' of the psalmist's life before he ever was, don't you think He knew what kind of father you were going to have?"

The girl stared at the text Mrs. Anderson had just read. "I guess He did."

"Rosie, I believe God had a purpose in allowing you to have the kind of a father you had."

Her eyes widened and her mouth opened.

"Now don't get me wrong, Rosie. I'm *not* saying that it was God's will that your father desert you and your mother. But I'm saying that God saw that it would happen and did not intervene to stop it because He knew that it could become a blessing to you—with the right attitude." Genny paused and waited for some response.

The anger had vanished from the girl's voice as she asked, "How can the type of father I had become a blessing to me?"

"He already has been a blessing to you, Rosie. Let me tell you how. You get almost straight A's in school. I wonder if you'd have been the high achiever you are if you would have had a father to lend complete security to your home. You're much more mature in your thinking, reasoning, and comprehension than most teens your age. I wonder if you would be so mature if you had not had to assist your mother and then great-aunt in running the house. And you're a natural leader. I've noticed that you are not dependent upon other kids your age. If you have something to say, you say it—without waiting to see if it's what your peers agree with. In fact, you don't seem to care if they *disagree* with you. I wonder if you'd express such independence if you had had a father to shield you from some of the blows of life.

"I see you as a unique individual that God wants to use. And I believe He saw that the circumstance of not having a father in your life would produce strengths of character in you that nothing else could.

"Now it's up to you. You can waste all the qualities God

has developed in you and use your uniqueness to turn people away from Him. Or you can use your qualities to lead your peers and others about you into a relationship with Him.

"You've got the independent quality, you've got the brains, and you've got the leadership ability. Now *you* have to decide what to do with them."

Silently Rosie stared out the windshield. Genny felt certain she had reached the core of Rosie's problem. "Rosie, let me share one more Bible text with you before I go. It's found in Hebrews 12:15. 'Watch out that no bitterness takes root among you, for as it springs up it causes deep trouble, hurting many in their spiritual lives' [T.L.B.]. Think about that text, Rosie. Is harboring a bitterness toward your father worth losing the blessings God has for you?"

Slowly the girl turned toward Genny. Mrs. Anderson could not remember a time when Rosie had been at a loss for words. "Rosie, why don't we bow our heads right now and thank God for the absence of a father figure in your life and then ask Him to turn your uniqueness into a blessing that will glorify His name?"

Rosie was serene as she replied, "I think I'd like to do that, Genny."

The next day was Sabbath. Mrs. Anderson didn't see the girl until the church service, but as Rosie entered the sanctuary Genny's face creased into a broad smile, for she was wearing a beautiful white and rose-flowered print dress—and it was *floor-length*. (Oddly enough, floor-length dresses were also in vogue during the 1970s.)

The motorcycle rides with her older boyfriend took more of a struggle to relinquish than her miniskirts, but she overcame them, too. And Rosie became a true Christian leader among her peers and in the Pathfinder Club. She ultimately received a college degree in business administration, and, after beginning her career in business, married a missionary teacher.

3

Thank God for a Suspended License

A solitary candle decorated each window of the six-teen-room house. Holly adorned the mantle of the stone fireplace in the living room, and on either side of the mantle stood two carved red candles. In the center of the mantle was an alabaster manger scene.

On the grand piano at one end of the long room was an enormous flower arrangement with a ribbon attached that read "Welcome Home, Mark." Gordon Stuart sat in an armchair next to the piano and stared at the ribbon and its message.

Mark had not been home to Lake George, New York, since he left for Harvard University in September, and Mr. Stuart had missed his son. Never before had he realized in such a poignant way how rapidly childhood turns into manhood. Gordon and Mark had gotten along well until the teen years—then something happened in their relation-ship. It seemed to Gordon that a wall had arisen between him and his son.

It had seemed so simple to raise Melissa, Mark's older sister. She and her mother had always been close, and he could just give them the checkbook and tell them to do whatever they wanted for the day and they were happy. The two of them would shop, go out to eat at some fancy restaurant, and maybe take in a movie or concert. Then at the first opportunity Melissa and his wife, Elizabeth, would put on a fashion show just for him. He would ooh and ah at how "enchanting" they looked in their new finery and feel he was fulfilling his role as a father. But Mark was a different matter.

Gordon thought of the time when his son was a freshman in high school competing in a countywide swim meet. The father had been present—at least *part* of the time. He had seen his son come in third and knew what a disappointment that was for the boy. Mark had been faithfully conditioning himself for weeks—watching his diet, swimming almost every day. And now, with his father watching him, he had finished only third.

Mr. Stuart could still see Mark standing at poolside, dripping wet with a towel flung about his shoulders, his head hanging low and his eyes fixed on the tile floor beneath his bare feet. Going up to him and putting his hand on his shoulder, the father had said, "That's OK, son; you're first in my book." Gordon remembered the look his son had given him. It said, "I don't believe you. If you really meant it, you'd cancel your business trip and spend the evening healing my wounded ego."

But Gordon had a plane to catch in forty-five minutes. He had recently begun his own financial counseling firm and was trying to make it a success. To get ahead, he must make sacrifices—at least that's what his philosophy *had* been.

But things had changed in Gordon's life. His doctor had recently diagnosed high blood pressure and an erratic heartbeat, and had prescribed a salt-free diet and an exercise program, along with some medication. And suddenly the luxurious home, the swimming pool, the two Cadillacs, and the country club membership didn't appear as important as it had in the past.

In addition, Gordon's wife had been attending some health programs and a family seminar sponsored by the Seventh-day Adventist Church. And what she had told him about the program was having an effect upon his thinking.

Elizabeth had been a good wife. She regularly attended

the Presbyterian church and had always taken the children to Sunday school. She was also a member of a weekly Bible study group that met in the homes of members on a rotation basis.

Gordon himself had been quite religious. But during recent years his work had become so demanding that he began to find it easier to sleep on Sunday mornings than go to church. While he still said a blessing before meals, family worship had been abandoned.

Feeling his need for reestablishing his relationship with Christ and his family, Gordon had looked forward to the Christmas holiday as a time when he and his son could become reacquainted with one another. Perhaps they could redeem some of the time they had lost.

Christmas wouldn't be quite the same this year. Melissa had married the previous spring and was in Saudi Arabia with her husband, an executive for a large oil company. Mark had called to say he would like to bring home a buddy, Jeff, for the holidays. At first Gordon was disappointed, but when his son explained that Jeff's parents had gone to Europe for the holidays and he would be alone unless he came home with Mark, Mr. Stuart agreed that the young man should accompany him.

Surely in a sixteen-room house a son and father ought to be able to find some place for a quiet talk, he thought.

"Don't you think it's time for you to shower and dress for dinner?" Elizabeth said as she suddenly entered the room. She was tall and slim and wore a red velvet floor-length skirt and a long-sleeved white satin blouse with softly ruffled collar and cuffs. Her frosted brown hair was short, and wisps of hair curled to frame her face.

Forty-five years old and still a beauty, Gordon thought as he arose from his chair to greet her. He took both her hands in his and kissed her.

Elizabeth looked purposefully at her husband. "You're apprehensive about tonight, aren't you, Gordon?" Her voice was soft and understanding.

"I never could hide anything from you, could I?"

"After twenty-four years of marriage, I guess I should know you pretty well, dear." Stepping closer to her husband, she put her arms around his waist. "I have a feeling this is going to be the most wonderful Christmas we've ever had. I've been praying about it, Gordon. I know how much this means to you, and I don't believe God will let us down."

Gently he pulled his wife into an embrace and placed his cheek against hers. "I don't know how God could turn down such a lovely petitioner."

Mark arrived home at 6:15 P.M. He requested and readily was granted a reprieve by Hazel, the cook, to delay serving the scheduled six-thirty dinner so that he and Jeff could freshen up. By seven, however, the family was seated around the dinner table—Mark at one end, Gordon at the other. Jeff and Elizabeth sat on either side.

"Did you two fellows enjoy your trip to Florida?" Mr. Stuart asked. (After they had finished their examinations, Mark and a group of his friends had taken a vacation to Daytona Beach, Florida, for a week before going to their respective homes. He and Jeff had driven together in Mark's El Dorado.)

"It was cooler than we had hoped—couldn't do much swimming. But we did get some sun," Mark said. Mark was a handsome young man with thick copper-colored hair. His every movement testified that he was athletic, yet he was quiet and somewhat reserved in nature.

"I have some friends near Daytona Beach," Jeff said, "and they told us where the best restaurants and night spots were." Of medium build, Jeff wore large wire-rimmed glasses that looked too big for his thin face.

"Night spots can get you into trouble," Gordon commented.

Nervously Mark looked at Jeff and then at his mother. "How are you feeling, Dad?"

"Not really too bad. Elizabeth and Hazel have been tending my diet like two watchdogs, and I've been trying to walk two miles each day. Walking really is quite enjoyable. Instead of scheduling business lunches with clients, I now usually eat a light lunch and then take a walk. It's amazing how refreshed I feel when I get back to the office. Often while I'm walking I get creative ideas, and many times when I arrive back in the office I have an answer for a perplexing situation that seemed unsolvable. It's unfortunate that I couldn't have discovered this before my health began to fade. I hope I've caught it in time. I've been a slave to my job far too long."

Unable to hide his look of surprise, Mark listened intently as his father spoke. Gordon could sense his son's astonishment.

"I think there would be an earthquake if I ever heard *my* father talk like that," Jeff observed. "He's a surgeon and a workaholic if I ever saw one."

The remainder of the conversation centered mostly on college life and classes. Both young men were doing well scholastically, and Mark said he was more certain than ever that he wanted to be an attorney.

Hazel's cheesecake with cherry topping was the rage of the evening. Though normally off-limits for Gordon's diet, Hazel and Elizabeth agreed he could have just a small sliver for the special occasion. After Mark's second piece he pushed his chair away from the table and said, "That was a delicious meal, but it sure hasn't helped keep me awake. We drove straight through from Daytona, and I'm beginning to feel all twenty-three hours of driving right now."

Elizabeth reached for her husband's arm. "Gordon, why don't you show Jeff to his room? I'm sure both he and Mark could use a good night's sleep. There'll be plenty of time for all of us to talk tomorrow."

Mr. Stuart arose from his seat. "The guest room overlooks Lake George, Jeff. I hope you'll like it."

The two young men both stood as Jeff said, "That sounds wonderful, Mr. Stuart. I have a penchant for water." He bade Mrs. Stuart and Mark Good night and left

27

with Gordon.

Mark walked to behind his mother's chair and placed both hands on her shoulders. "It's good to be home, Mom."

Elizabeth turned to look at her son and took his left hand in hers. "It's good to have you home, Mark. The house seems quite empty with both you and Melissa gone. Surprisingly enough, I even miss the spats you and she used to have."

Her son laughed, but his laughter was tense.

Mrs. Stuart's face grew serious. "Mark, is something bothering you? I know you're tired from the long trip, but you seem somewhat nervous tonight. Are your studies straining you?"

"I'm just tired, Mother," he quickly replied. "I'll be good as new tomorrow." Patting her hand, he kissed her on the cheek and left the room.

Mark's bedroom was on the second floor at the opposite end of the hall from the guest room. As he arrived at his room his father had just finished saying Good night to Jeff and was walking toward him.

As Gordon approached his son he could feel himself tense, though he consciously tried to sound relaxed as he said, "It's good having you home, Mark."

The son appeared tense too. He looked at the floor, then at his father. "Dad, there's something I have to get off my chest. I was going to put it off until tomorrow, but . . . can we talk for a few minutes now?"

Gordon could feel a warm excitement well up inside him. He had hoped to spend some time alone with his son, but now that the occasion had arrived, he felt his palms becoming moist and could feel his face flush.

Why am I so nervous? he thought. I've negotiated with bank presidents, huge corporation executives, oil magnates, and even some internationally known celebrities. Why am I apprehensive about talking to my own son?

Despite all the control he could muster, his voice quivered slightly as he managed to say, "Sure, son. Let's go into your room.''

Gordon took a seat in the overstuffed chair to the left of his son's bed. Mark seated himself on the left side of the bed, facing his father. Striving to project a relaxed voice, Gordon asked, "Is something troubling you, Mark?"

"Yes, it's been eating away at me for two weeks now, and regardless of how you'll feel about it, I've got to tell you.'' He rubbed his hands against his corduroy slacks, and Gordon knew that Mark's palms must also be sweating.

"What is it? Are you in trouble?" He leaned toward Mark.

His son responded quickly. "No! I mean, yes . . .'' Mark wiped his hands on his thighs once more and then blurted out, "I've had my driver's license suspended for reckless driving.'' As he awaited his father's response, he looked down at his lap.

Gordon paused a moment, then said, "Was it some mistake, or were you at fault?"

Briefly Mark glanced at his father, then lowered his head. "I was at fault. I was showing off how well the El Dorado handles. I had three buddies with me, and I did some pretty fancy driving. I thought of not telling you, but you'll find out soon enough, because the car insurance will be increased significantly and I know the insurance payment is due after the first of the year.''

Mr. Stuart's face reddened. "You mean you deliberately drove recklessly? Don't you realize that you could have killed someone, or been killed yourself? What would have happened if you'd have been responsible for the death of one of your buddies, or some innocent person driving another car?''

Again Mark rubbed his hands against his thighs and managed to interject, "I know it was dumb.''

"Dumb? It was downright foolish! Haven't we taught you that a car can be a dangerous weapon when mishandled? Driving is a privilege, not some kind of kid's game.'' Abruptly he stopped and stared at his son. "Where did this happen?''

"In Cambridge, near the university."

"Then who drove the El Dorado to Daytona?"

"Jeff did mostly. I drove only when he got too tired."

The vein in Gordon's temple looked ready to pop as he rose from his chair. "You mean you drove without a license? Don't you know that if something happened people could bring suit against me? All that I've worked for could be in jeopardy. People are lawsuit-minded these days. You're studying to be a lawyer—you know how often people sue and for how *much*."

Mr. Stuart began pacing in front of his son. "You're ungrateful, Mark. Your mother and I have sacrificed and worked hard to get where we are. We send you to Harvard, give you an El Dorado, the best clothes, and anything else you ask for, and *this* is how you repay us."

The young man's face tensed. "What are you trying to do, make a federal case out of this? Nothing serious happened, and I'm sorry. What else do you want me to do?"

Gordon whirled and looked at him. "Nothing serious happened? You're sorry? How can you be sorry when you deliberately drive without a license all the way to Daytona Beach?"

"I didn't drive all the way to Daytona. I *told* you Jeff drove most of the way," Mark yelled.

"Don't talk to *me* in that tone of voice. Remember, I'm your father."

Mark stared down at his corduroy slacks and his hands resumed rubbing his thighs.

"We've given you too much. From now on things are going to be different, young man. You're going back to school by plane or bus, but no car. And I'll expect you to get a job and pay for your *own* car insurance from now on."

Stomping out of the bedroom, Gordon slammed the door behind him. Once outside, he paused for a moment. What have I done? he thought. This wasn't the way it was supposed to be. I looked forward to Mark's coming home so we could establish communication and develop a closer relationship. Drops of perspiration outlined his forehead as he turned back toward the bedroom door. He began to reach for the doorknob, but stopped short. If I apologize, he thought, I'll be going back on my word. And I *do* believe Mark needs to feel more responsibility. Besides, he'd see me as weak and vacillating. What kind of example is that for a son? Slowly his hand lowered to his side. After staring at Mark's door for a moment, he quickly turned and walked away.

Elizabeth was reading in bed as Gordon entered their bedroom. "This holiday is going to be a disaster," he said as he walked to her side of the bed and sat down.

She laid the open book she was reading upside down on the bed. "What's wrong?"

"I've just had an argument with Mark." Then he proceeded to relate to her what had happened.

After her initial shock and some pensive thinking, she responded. "You were right in laying down some guidelines for Mark to help him feel more responsibility, Gordon. I've realized as I've been attending the family seminar at the Adventist Church that we have probably been lax in helping our children accept responsibilities. I thought it was too late to do anything about it, but perhaps it isn't."

Her husband rose from the bed and walked over to the sliding glass doors that led to a veranda overlooking the lake. Pulling aside the drapes, he stared out at the night. "Well, if I did the right thing, why do I feel so rotten about it all?" he retorted.

Elizabeth threw back the covers, got out of bed, and walked around to his side. She took one of his hands, and he responded by turning toward her. As she spoke she searched his eyes. "It's not so much *what* you said, but the *way* you said it that's bothering you, honey."

Still holding his hand, she directed him to a love seat perpendicular to the sliding doors. Once seated, she looked intently at him. "Mark's behavior strikes at both of us, Gordon. Looking into my own heart, I can see myself saying, 'How could *my* son have done such a careless, ridiculous thing?' To be very honest, Gordon, my *pride* is hurt. I'd like to think I did a better job of raising him than that."

Her husband remained silent as she continued. "I've come to realize while attending this seminar that other parents feel this same sense of hurt when their children perform contrary to their expectations. As Christians we are aware that there is nothing we can do about the past. We might feel guilty about things we could have done better, but that feeling is not going to help the present or the future unless we take positive action."

"That's where I've already blown it," Gordon said. "I've already responded negatively to Mark."

"You may have, but that doesn't mean that all is lost. I believe God is well able to turn any seeming disaster in a Christian's life into a blessing, and I believe He can transform this situation into the very thing you have been desiring—namely, a closer relationship with our son."

"How, Elizabeth?" his expression was one of bewilderment. "If I apologize, he'll think everything can go back to the way it's been—me paying the bills and him taking advantage of it all."

"You're right about one thing, Gordon; I do think you should apologize—"

He interrupted abruptly, "I can't. Don't you see . . . ?"

Elizabeth put her index finger to his lips. "Now don't get excited, dear." With an impish smile she continued, "Let me finish, and *then* you can tell me how crazy I am, OK?" She chuckled, and her calmness disarmed her husband and he grew quiet. "I don't believe you should apologize for telling Mark that he must cease driving until his license is returned, or that he must now pay for his own car insurance. I believe you have done the right thing there. But as Christians, we do have a responsibility to apologize for the wrong that we have committed in any given situation. And I think you would find Mark's respect for you would grow enormously if you would apologize for the *way* you approached the problem."

Gordon kept his gaze averted as he spoke, "Mark looked like a battered puppy as I yelled at him. Why couldn't I have had your cool head around while I was verbally abusing my son? It's not my intention to hurt him. I want to help him. And most of all I want him to realize that I want to be his friend." His voice broke, and he reached in his back pocket for a handkerchief to wipe his eyes.

Cupping her husband's face in her hands, Elizabeth kissed him. "I know you want that, darling. Why don't we pray about this situation right now and ask God to make something beautiful out of it?"

They both knelt beside the love seat, each petitioning God in behalf of Mark. When they arose from prayer, Gordon said, "It's going to be hard, Elizabeth, but I'm going back to his room right now."

Mr. Stuart knocked on Mark's door. When there was no response, he knocked again and called through the door, "Mark, it's Dad. Can I come in, son?"

Gordon heard movement in the room, and in a moment his son opened the door. Mark stood in his stocking feet. After his father entered the room, the young man thrust his hands deep in his pants pockets. Just like he used to when he'd been caught doing something wrong, Gordon thought. How like a little boy he looks . . . a little big boy.

Mark stared down at the floor, and his father noticed he was standing on the outside edges of his stocking feet. Suddenly Gordon became aware of his own awkward feeling and cleared his throat. Then he began to speak in a slow, quiet tone. "I want to apologize to you for losing my temper, son."

Mark raised his head to glance at his father. His eyes were wide and his lips slightly parted as his father continued speaking in a calm voice.

"I want you to know, Mark, that this doesn't mean that I'm removing the penalty for your frivolous act. But it does mean that your father is deeply sorry for the way he spoke to you. Will you forgive me?"

Silent for a moment, Mark seemed to be groping for words. When they finally came they were halting. "I—I'm the one that's at fault, Dad. I know I've disappointed you and Mother." He walked to the overstuffed chair and faced the window, his back toward his father. "You had reason to be angry. I've been unappreciative of what you've done for me."

Gordon stepped up behind his son and put his hands on the young man's broad shoulders. "Mark, I think perhaps we've both been unappreciative of each other. Only you have a better excuse than I have—I'm supposed to be old enough to know better."

Mr. Stuart sat on the edge of his son's bed. "Mark, come here and sit next to me." He gestured, and Mark sat beside him.

"It's easy for a father to start taking a son, and a family, for granted. You'll find, as I did, that the business world is a rat race. It's so easy to fall into a pattern of material things and to strive for success and acclaim. But believe me, Mark, there is nothing out there in the world that is more rewarding or fulfilling than what is happening between us right now. I wouldn't trade this for all the money in the world. And let me say this, Mark, it's not my intention to hurt you in any way by telling you that I expect you to pay for your own car insurance. My sincere intention is for your good."

"I've been thinking about that, Dad. I think I'd not only like to pay for my own car insurance"—he hesitated—"but I'd like to earn enough money to buy my own car."

"Mark, you're kidding. You could never earn enough money at a part-time job to buy a car equal to the El Dorado you've been driving."

"I know that, Dad. It's just that all my life you've given me every material thing I could ever wish for. I don't want to sound unappreciative, but now I would really like to be able to point to something and say, 'This is what *I've* worked for, and it's all mine,' even if it's a used Ford or

Chevy. I can't tell you why I feel that way, Dad. It's just something that I need to do."

His father was silent for a moment. "I think I understand, Mark," he said finally, then turned to look at his son as he continued. "You've become a man, and one your dad is mighty proud of."

Mark smiled, but Gordon saw some little-boy tears come to his son's eyes. He could feel his own eyes begin to smart as he put his arm around his son's shoulder and asked, "Mark, I haven't done this with you for some years now, but would you like to have a word of prayer with your dad? This dad sure needs your prayers."

The young man smiled broadly. "And this son sure needs yours—I've never had a job before." Both chuckled, and then Mark slipped his arm around his father and the two bowed their heads and prayed for each other.

After prayer both men embraced, and each noticed the other's eyes were moist. Gordon grinned as he wiped his eyes with his handkerchief. "I won't tell anyone we were crying if you won't."

Mark laughed aloud and held out his right hand to his father. "That's a deal, Dad."

4

Thank God for a Lost Temper

I t had only been six months since John Schindler had been assigned to the two-church district in southern Michigan as pastor, but already the largest of the two churches was filled each Sabbath morning. On a number of Sabbaths, the deacons had to place extra chairs in the sanctuary to accommodate those attending.

In addition to his good preaching, John had begun training his church members to give Bible studies. Each Monday evening John, his wife, Pat, and other members experienced in giving Bible studies, each took an inexperienced person with them to a home and presented an actual study. In time, the individual obtained confidence, became active in the study, and began training another inexperienced church member to give studies. In this manner the Bible study teams were growing, and so was the church.

Pat was proud of her husband. She and John had been married only a few months, he had just been recently ordained, and their future looked bright.

On one particular Sabbath morning Pat found herself with no responsibilities in any of the children's division Sabbath schools where she normally assisted, and she thought she would attend one of the adult classes for a change.

Pat chose one of the three classes in the sanctuary and sat in the front row of the class taught by Mr. Russell. The discussion revolved around how to make worship more meaningful. One class member responding to the subject, suggested the heart should be prepared all week in order to enjoy true worship on Sabbath. Another mentioned the necessity of studying the Sabbath school lesson faithfully in order to be able to contribute to the lesson study as well as to obtain more from the group discussion. Still another gave hints on how parents could prepare their children to have a proper attitude in church.

Suddenly Madelyn Jeffries, the church organist, spoke up. "I feel we have far too much sermonizing in church." Her voice sounded self-assured and somewhat defiant. "I think we should have less preaching and turn the time into testimony periods."

Pat felt her cheeks flush slightly but tried to appear unruffled. John had requested personal testimonies after a short sermonette just a few weeks earlier. Was Madelyn suggesting that should be done routinely?

Mr. Russell, sensing the developing tension, tried to divert the discussion into a more positive channel. "Some testimonies are nice," he said kindly, "but I'm sure none of us would want a testimony period every week." With a nervous smile he attempted to go on with the lesson. However, Madelyn interrupted him.

"Oh, I don't know; it seems to me *that* would be far more beneficial to the congregation than hearing sermon after sermon week after week."

Mr. Russell glanced quickly at Pat, who changed positions in her seat, crossed her legs, and struggled to maintain her composure. She could feel the man's uneasiness and sensed other members of the class beginning to feel unnerved.

Madelyn had a reputation for being critical and faultfinding. Several members had warned the Schindlers about her, but so far they had managed to stay on good terms with her. As a matter of fact, Pat and John had her on their prayer list. Many of the church members didn't like her, and the pastor and his wife were praying that God would work in her life so that the congregation would find her more lovable.

Both Pat and John had encouraged Madelyn to help them with their Bible study teams. They felt that if she would join with them in witnessing, the experience would help her own critical attitude, and the association would give the Schindlers an opportunity to get close to her. Madelyn always said she planned to help, but then never came on Monday nights. Finally the Schindlers had decided that the best thing they could do was to give her unqualified love and acceptance.

But now Pat felt herself becoming intimidated, and she silently prayed for grace to endure the negative comments the woman was making.

"In addition to too much sermonizing," Madelyn continued, "we don't do enough to get members active in giving Bible studies. Members just can't be spoon-fed all the time; they have to be weaned so they can win *other* souls."

Her words cut Pat to the core. That's the very thing we're doing, she thought to herself. What in the world is she talking about?

Before Pat realized what she was doing, she turned around to face Madelyn, who was sitting in the pew in back of her, and said in a tone cloaked in winter wind, "Where are *you* on Monday nights, Madelyn?"

To her surprise, the woman withered before her eyes. Madelyn tried to speak and began to stutter. "I—I—I've intended to come, but i—i—it seems I'm always busy."

In the same chilled tone but with an added note of sarcasm, Pat said, "Tell us all about it, Madelyn." Then she turned forward in her seat and sat rigid. Somewhere she could hear Mr. Russell nervously clearing his throat and muttering, "We must get on with the lesson study class; our time's almost up."

Pat felt as if isolated on an island—totally oblivious to anything else said in class. How could I have lost my temper like that? she demanded of herself. And to the very person John and I have been praying for. What kind of witness have I been? How can I expect this congregation to love Madelyn when *I* can't?

It all had happened so fast. She would have never thought herself capable of retorting so rudely—and in front of a whole Sabbath school class! Inwardly Pat cringed.

"Oh, God," she prayed silently, "I'm so sorry for attacking one of Your children. I don't know what You can do with this mess, but Lord, I give it to You. I know You can make something good out of our worst mistakes. Please take control of this situation and glorify Your name through it all."

No sooner had she finished her prayer than she remembered that it was communion Sabbath. "Oh, Lord, how can I partake of the emblems of Your broken body and spilled blood when I have just offended one whom You died to save?"

Immediately the thought came, You must ask Madelyn's forgiveness. It was your pride in your husband's accomplishments that she wounded when she made some negative comments. And it was lack of love for her that made you lash out at her in public. You know what the Bible says in Matthew 18:15 about telling your brother "his fault between thee and him alone." Madelyn may have been wrong in criticizing, but you must live by Biblical principles even though others may not. You must apologize for *your* wrong acts whether or not she ever realizes hers.

At the end of Sabbath school, Pat, still somewhat dazed, rose slowly to her feet. She turned to look for Madelyn and saw her at the rear of the sanctuary, near the exit. Hurriedly Mrs. Schlinder walked to the back of the church and caught Madelyn's arm just as she reached the sanctuary doors.

The woman turned, and when she saw the minister's wife, she avoided looking directly into her eyes. "Madelyn, will you forgive me for my pride and lack of love?" Pat's eyes mirrored her concern.

Mrs. Jeffries stared at her as if her ears were questioning

what she was hearing. Finally, slowly, quietly, the words began to come. "I—I must have offended you . . ."

Mrs. Schlinder looked straight into Madelyn's eyes as she pleaded, "Will you forgive me?"

A confused expression crossed the other woman's face as she stammered, "Sure . . . sure, I'll forgive you." Then she turned abruptly and left.

Madelyn didn't stay for church that day. The substitute organist played for the worship and communion service. Pat felt certain it was because of her that Mrs. Jeffries had left church.

All week long Pat prayed for Madelyn whenever she thought of her. But the next Sabbath Mrs. Jeffries was absent from church too. The following week Pat and John wrestled with whether or not to visit her or to just allow her a little more time to cool off. They decided to wait one more week before trying to contact her.

The next Sabbath Madelyn was back at her post as church organist. She seems so cheerful, Pat thought. She's taking the initiative in saying Hello to fellow members this morning instead of complaining about them not greeting her.

After the worship service Mrs. Jeffries was the last person to greet the Schlinders as they stood at the door saying Goodbye to the worshipers. As Madelyn approached Pat she said, "I didn't stay for the communion service two weeks ago because I didn't feel my heart was right." The woman looked at the floor a moment and then continued. "Last week I wasn't here because I traveled several miles to another church where I knew they were having communion. I partook of communion last week because I've learned that I've been too critical. But I believe I've learned now that we are one body in Christ, and that our duty as Christians is to edify one another, not tear one another down."

Pat learned something too—that God can take a lost temper and use it to glorify His name.

5

Thank God for Rigid Rules

Bev Collins hummed softly as she paused from kneading bread dough to look out at the vibrant fall colors. The morning sun illuminated the crimson leaves of the red maple tree just outside the kitchen window, promising another perfect autumn day.

There must be time for a walk by the river today, she thought.

The ringing of the telephone abruptly ended her daydreaming, and she quickly wiped her hands and reached for the receiver of her wall phone.

"Good morning, Collins residence."

"Bev—this is Shirley." The voice at the other end of the line broke into sobbing.

As a minister's wife, Bev had received other tearful calls, but most of them had been from emotionally fragile people. Shirley Morrow was a stable, positive-minded housewife. Her husband, Dan, had a similar disposition and was a successful sales manager.

The two teenage Morrow boys, John, 14, and Rich, 18, were wholesome and well mannered. Bev and her husband, Bill, had always found it refreshing to visit their home. Laughter and hospitality overflowed in it. The two boys always seemed to be involved in some new and interesting project. In addition to their part-time jobs, the boys built models, helped their dad with various household repairs, and participated in neighborhood sports with

41

their friends. John loved to play the piano.

Shirley and Dan took a lot of interest in their sons, and one could often find Dan in the fray of a touch football game. Shirley enjoyed having the boys' friends over and was accustomed to making meals for several—always in her relaxed, informal manner.

Bev's mind whirled as she stood holding the receiver. Had something happened to Dan or one of the boys? Fighting to maintain a controlled voice, she asked, "Shirley, what's wrong?"

"They're sending John home from academy." Mrs. Morrow's voice faded. Bev waited silently while she gained composure enough to continue.

"He's been suspended for smoking marijuana, and the boys' dean is bringing him home this afternoon. That's all the information the dean would give me by phone. He said he'd discuss the details when he arrives."

The news stunned Bev. It was John's first year at a church-operated boarding school, and he had been looking forward to attending. Shirley and Dan were dedicated Christians who were concerned about the spiritual and intellectual development of their children, and had elected to send both boys through their church's school system, even though it meant the boys would have to live away from home during their secondary education. Rich had recently graduated from the same academy John was now attending, and was currently enrolled in a local hospital's medical technician program.

In Bev's estimation, no young man could have been better prepared, or had a better attitude about going away to school, than John.

"Oh, Shirley, I'm so sorry. Is there anything we can do?"

"Dan is out of town, and I won't be able to reach him until tonight. John and Dean Manner will be here at two o'clock this afternoon. I don't think I can handle this alone. Could you and Bill please be here?"

"Of course, Shirley. Would you like us to come a little

earlier so we'll be sure to be there when they arrive?"

"I'd really appreciate that."

"Bill's at the church office. I'll call him right now. We'll be at your place by one-thirty." Mrs. Collins paused, then decided to add, "Shirley, this may sound odd right now, but remember that 'all things work together for good to them that love God.' He has a blessing hidden in this somewhere."

At 1:32 P.M. Pastor and Mrs. Collins knocked at the front door of the Morrow home. Shirley's red eyes displayed her anguish, but she managed to smile as they entered the living room. "Thanks so much for coming."

The Collins's took their customary seats. Bill tried to settle back in the relaxed position that this home normally encouraged, but Bev noticed how awkward he looked. She herself sat rigidly at the edge of her chair, her face serious.

Bill leaned forward. His brow creased as he spoke. "Shirley, do you want to talk about what you're feeling right now?"

"I guess I'm feeling resentment, Bill. After all, neither of our boys has ever been in any trouble before, and I can't help thinking the school is being rigid and unfair in their handling of this. Why can't they just give John a warning for a first offense?" Anger flared from her eyes as she spoke.

His voice deliberately calm and low, Bill replied. "I can understand what you're feeling, Shirley. Any parent would feel the same way given a similar situation. But let's follow your train of thought to its conclusion, shall we?"

Mrs. Morrow nodded as she momentarily looked down at the hankie in her hand.

"We all know one of the rules of the academy is that anyone found smoking marijuana will be immediately suspended. Now suppose that when John comes home you make it quite clear that you feel the school is, as you say, being 'rigid and unfair' in its dealing with him. What will you be telling John about rules and authority?"

Bev prayed silently as she watched Shirley's expression.

The tense, furrowed brow relaxed as Mrs. Morrow replied, "I guess I'd be telling him that the rules should be changed for him."

"Exactly. Now what kind of a foundation does that lay for him in future situations when he is confronted with other rules and regulations he disagrees with? How will he respond to rules regarding his employment, or marriage responsibilities, or the laws of the land, or even the law of God?"

"I see what you're saying, Bill. But this sure is a hard pill to swallow."

"I know it's not easy right now, but in the long run, backing the authority of the school will pay you richer dividends than rejecting their authority before your son. In fact, Shirley, God's Word teaches us that sometimes even if we are dealt with wrongfully, it is more noble to submit to authority. Let me read to you 1 Peter 2:18, 19, and 21 to 23 out of The New English Bible: 'Servants, accept the authority of your masters with all due submission, not only when they are kind and considerate, but even when they are perverse. For it is a fine thing if a man endure the pain of undeserved suffering because God is in his thoughts.' 'To that you were called, because Christ suffered on your behalf, and thereby left you an example; it is for you to follow in his steps. He committed no sin, he was convicted of no falsehood; when he was abused he did not retort with abuse, when he suffered he uttered no threats, but committed his cause to the One who judges justly.'

"How about you entrusting your son to Him who judges justly, Shirley? If you do, God will be able to make something beautiful even out of this situation."

A serenity now radiated from Mrs. Morrow. "As you've been talking, the words Bev quoted to me by phone earlier have been running through my mind. 'All things work together for good to them that love God.' Where is that text found, Bev?"

"Romans 8:28, Shirley. And I believe God is going to work this all out for good too, don't you?"

"Maybe so, Bev."

They heard the sound of a car door. Bev glanced out the living room window. "They're here," she announced.

Dean Manner entered the room with John and another young man also being suspended for the same offense. Mrs. Morrow sent the boys to the basement recreation room while she spoke with the dean.

After proper introductions, Shirley invited Dean Manner to take a seat on the couch. The dean's voice was unsteady as he spoke. "I'm terribly sorry for what has happened, Mrs. Morrow. I want you to know that the academy feels that John is a fine boy, but he didn't use discretion in choosing his friends. He was found smoking marijuana with some students who do not have the same attitude as your son. Unfortunately the school can't judge pupils on attitude alone, and must wait until some rule is broken before it can take any legitimate action."

In a calm tone she asked, "Did you actually *see* my son smoking marijuana?"

The dean looked down at the floor, then straight into her eyes. "I'm afraid so, Mrs. Morrow."

Shirley fought against her tears but lost the battle.

Bill now entered the conversation. "Dean Manner, what does this mean as far as John's future attendance at your academy is concerned?"

"Well, of course, he cannot return to school this year, but next fall he can apply again."

Shirley, regaining control, asked, "What are his chances for reentry next fall?"

"If he keeps out of trouble and has good recommendations, his chances should be very good. John is deeply sorry for this offense, Mrs. Morrow. If you and your husband support the school in this decision, I feel you're going to have a stronger son as a result."

"The pastor and his wife were just telling me something similar. I'm beginning to believe it." Shirley's face creased into a beautiful smile.

After returning from his business trip and a similar

internal struggle to that of his wife's, Dan Morrow accepted the school's decision. Then the Morrows enrolled their son in a local public high school.

To demonstrate their personal disapproval of John's action, his parents allowed him to go only to classes, a weekly piano lesson, and church for one month. They permitted no outside entertainment—even banning television for that period of time.

A week and a half after John's return, the Collins's visited the Morrow home again. As they entered the living room they could sense a degree of normalcy returning. The only element of tension came from John's quietness as he sat on the edge of the piano bench facing the four adults. His usual eagerness to share his most recent endeavor with the Collins's was absent.

Bill looked at him and beamed a warm smile in his direction. "Well, how are things going for you, John?"

The teenager looked down at the floor and began swinging his right foot back and forth. "All right," he said softly.

Bev could wait no longer to share an idea of hers with John and his family. "John, we've got a bit of a problem at church, and we're wondering if you'd consider helping us?"

His head raised quickly and he looked attentively at Bev. His eyes showed quizzical surprise. "What kind of problem?"

"Well, as you know, our choir has already begun practice for the Christmas concert. We only have one pianist in the church, and she often must be out of town. So we've had to practice without an accompanist on recent occasions. That isn't easy for a volunteer choir that basically doesn't read music. Now, we were wondering if you'd consider being our assistant pianist. In fact, we need you for this week's practice."

John looked at his parents, then back at Bev, his dark-brown eyes bright and wide. "I'd be glad to help . . . if it's OK with my parents."

Bev and Bill looked at Mr. and Mrs. Morrow, who were radiant with smiles. Dan glanced at his wife as he spoke. "I think that could be arranged. How about it, Shirley?"

Shirley beamed as she responded, "I'd love to see him do it."

In the ensuing months John did play for the choir. His musical skills became so proficient that he accompanied the choir publicly many times, and presented solo compositions as well for the worship service. The choir and church members in general praised him enthusiastically.

The year passed quickly, and the following fall the academy from which he had been suspended once again accepted him. This time, however, John became immediately involved in the school choir. As students and faculty became aware of his musical ability, they inundated him with requests to play for morning worships and as accompanist for various singing and instrumental groups.

John progressed well in school that year and the following two years. During the last half of his senior year, he sent a letter to his parents. Three paragraphs were particularly significant to them:

"My senior year is rapidly coming to a close. Before it ends I want you to know how very much I appreciate all you have done for me. I know the cost of my schooling has been a sacrifice for you. And I want to thank you for caring enough about me to make that sacrifice.

"Thanks too for not giving up on me when I blew the first year.

"I've been thinking and praying a lot about what I want to do for a life's work. I'm not real sure yet, but I want it to be in a field where I can help other people—perhaps a minister, a doctor, or maybe a boys' dean."

Shirley wiped her eyes as she handed the letter to Dan to finish reading. As she did so, she managed to blubber out from a tear-blotched face, "Thank God for rigid rules."

6

Thank God for Cancer

The clock on the dresser read 3:00 A.M. Sleep unattainable, Sheri Shaffer stared into the blackness. Quiet tears slipped out the corners of her eyes and onto her pillow. "Please, God," she prayed, "give me the assurance that Mom and Dad have eternal life."

Her husband, Wally, and she had just returned to Kentucky from a visit to her parents' home in Indiana, and she was troubled. Something was wrong—something an only child can sense before anyone else.

Her parents' preoccupation with "things," their critical attitude of the church, their argumentative comments regarding vegetarianism, and the derogatory statements about their local pastor had left a hollow in her heart. Every effort toward positive religious conversation had seemed to end in failure. Sheri felt frustrated, depressed, and defeated.

Wally had merely written the experience off with a "Don't take things so seriously, honey; that's just the way your folks are." But she knew better. Something within kept saying, "Pray for your parents."

Four months later on a hot August evening, the telephone rang. It was Dad.

"Mom will be having surgery later this week. Nothing serious; the doctor calls it a fatty tumor. It's on her thigh."

Immediately Sheri made flight arrangements. She would be there for the surgery and remain to assist with her mother's recovery.

The evening of her arrival in Indiana, after visiting her mother in the hospital, Sheri and her father spoke with the doctor. He informed them that the "fatty tumor" was actually fibrosarcoma, a slow-growing cancer. He said that the tumor was large and deep, and that the operation at best would leave Mrs. Shaffer with a limp, useless leg. His suggestion was to amputate the leg and part of the hip in hope that it would spare her life.

Sheri was stunned; her father was upset and angry with the doctor. Why hadn't he been told of this sooner? At the same time she tried to calm her father, Sheri struggled to convince herself that there was hope. "Don't worry, Dad. God has a plan and a reason."

That night as Sheri walked up the stairs to the room she had occupied while still single and living at home, her heart felt hollow. Her steps were labored, and she had to force each foot to move.

It's amazing how different a room looks when you know the person who has readied it for you is facing death, she thought. The bedspread, the doilies, the spinning wheel lamp, the silk doll upon the bed all cried out, "Mother." The courageous facade was over. In anguish Sheri slumped on the floor in front of the window she had always prayed before while living at home—her prayer window. Now, without looking out at the blackness of the night, she began praying silently through a torrent of tears: "Why, God, why? Mother is so active. To take a leg away from her would be worse than death to her. I've prayed that You would give me the assurance that my parents have eternal life—now are You going to take Mother away without giving me that, and leave Dad bitter and angry? Is *this* how You answer my prayer? . . . Or is this really the only way You can fulfill my prayer? Oh, God, help me to have strength enough—faith enough—to trust You."

Sheri prayed and read Scripture almost the entire night, searching her heart, petitioning God for what to do. The doctor had advised her not to tell Mrs. Shaffer about the cancer. In his estimation her mother would not be emotionally able to cope with the truth. The daughter disagreed.

As far back as Sheri could remember, her mother had been a praying mother, a mother with strong faith—an imperfect and very human mother, to be sure, but one for whose prayers Sheri had always had great respect. And Sheri believed that source of strength was still there to be tapped.

The next morning Sheri telephoned the doctor. "What if we don't operate?" The physician replied that they could try cobalt treatments to see if they could shrink or at least arrest the tumor, but he urged surgery.

After Sheri consulted with her father, both agreed the cobalt therapy was worth attempting. The doctor would make arrangements to begin it as soon as possible, and Mrs. Shaffer would receive treatment as an outpatient.

Mr. Shaffer was sullen as he and his daughter traveled to the hospital that morning to bring Mrs. Shaffer home. Only once did he break the silence to say, "What a way to end thirty-four years of marriage."

Sheri knew her father was feeling the same devastation that she did. The cobalt treatments were an option that held *little* hope, but they still held hope. She tried to sound as positive as she could force her voice to be as she responded to her father's statement. "It's possible that the cobalt treatments can help, Dad."

"Should we tell Mother it's cancer?" her father asked.

Hearing the word "cancer" was almost like hearing a death knell. So little is known about this disease, she thought. Her body tensed as she responded. "I wouldn't volunteer the information, Dad, but if Mother asks me, I will not lie to her."

Her father's jaw tightened as she spoke, but his eyes remained firmly on the road in front of him.

Mrs. Shaffer was chatting with a fellow patient in the bed next to hers when her husband and daughter arrived. She seemed in good spirits and was surprised and delighted when she learned she was going home and that she would have radiation therapy instead of surgery. Quickly dressing, she gathered up her few hospital items and said Goodbye to her roommate. As Mrs. Shaffer walked down the corridor she waved Goodbye to a patient in the next room with whom she had become acquainted. The patient called out, "Where are you going?" And Mrs. Shaffer responded with a cheerful, "I'm going home."

"Going home." The words resounded and reechoed in Sheri's mind. The cheeriness with which her mother spoke only added to the gloom surrounding Sheri. Oh, God, she thought, if Mother knew the truth, what would it do to her? She's so naive; she doesn't suspect a thing.

Her mother chattered about the woman who had roomed with her. She was recovering from a mastectomy. "They're not sure they got it all," Mrs. Shaffer said. "But she doesn't know that. Her husband told me. Poor soul."

Sheri's legs felt like rubber appendages. A fist-size lump had taken residence in her stomach, but she managed a mechanical smile as one of the nurses nodded a friendly farewell.

As she sat in the back seat of the car, Sheri felt thankful for a few minutes to gain composure before having to look her mother in the eye. She must hide her concern, and it was easier to do by voice than by facial expression. Mother always seemed to be able to read messages hidden in her face.

A few minutes were all that she had, for as soon as Mr. Shaffer got into the driver's seat, Mrs. Shaffer began asking questions. "It sure is good to get out of that hospital. I *hate* hospitals . . . By the way, what kind of treatments am I going to have?"

Sheri's body tensed, but to her relief her father began to answer the question. "It's called cobalt therapy. As I understand it, rays are directed into the tumor by means of a machine. The rays are suppose to shrink the tumor."

"That's wonderful!" Mrs. Shaffer replied. Her body seemed to relax as she took a deep breath. "Well, at least it's not cancer."

Neither Mr. Shaffer nor Sheri responded to her statement. The long pause of silence that followed said it all.

Mrs. Shaffer abruptly leaned forward in her seat and looked straight at her husband. Her eyes were large and her forehead furrowed. "Is it cancer? Is it?"

Mr. Shaffer said nothing. He stared straight ahead at the road as if chiseled out of stone.

Turning to glance at her daughter, Mrs. Shaffer asked, "Is it cancer?"

Sheri felt a numbness begin in the center of her chest and radiate to her arms. She was hardly aware that her lips were moving, but she heard the words slowly, quietly come from somewhere within her, "Yes, Mother."

A look of surprised astonishment came to her mother's face.

"These cobalt treatments are rather new, and they've had some good success with them," Sheri heard herself saying.

Mrs. Shaffer glanced at her husband. "The doctor said it was a fatty tumor and that these tumors are never malignant."

Mr. Shaffer turned to look at his wife. "That's what he told me, honey. He didn't tell me it was cancer until Sheri arrived here."

"Why didn't he tell me?" At the moment Mrs. Shaffer seemed more upset with being betrayed than with the disease.

Sheri explained that the doctor had felt she would not be able to cope with the truth and had kept it from her to prevent her unnecessary trauma. As Sheri spoke, she watched her mother's face. "I did not agree with the doctor, Mother. I told him that you are a Christian and that your faith in God is sufficient to see you through this ordeal." An expression of serenity came to her mother's face.

As the ride progressed, the father and daughter laid out the alternatives open to Mrs. Shaffer with regard to her condition. She too agreed that she should try the cobalt treatments. "I would rather die than lose my leg," she said.

Mrs. Shaffer returned from the hospital on a Friday. That evening, just as the sun began to set, a gentle rain fell and left in its wake the most vivid rainbow Sheri and her parents had ever seen. The rainbow formed a perfect arc and appeared at the end of the field next to the Shaffers' country home. The distant trees shimmered with silver and gold hues, and the grass in the field sparkled with raindrop diamonds. At the sight, the three family members rushed outside to allow the awesome beauty to envelop them.

"Mother," Sheri said, "I believe God put on this display just for you. That's the rainbow of His promise. I believe He's telling you that you can trust Him to see you through this difficult time."

Mrs. Shaffer's eyes remained fixed on the rainbow as she said, "I believe you're right, Sheri."

The daughter's heart was at peace as she journeyed home to Kentucky. Surely, she thought, God was using the experience to rekindle the beautiful Christian experience her parents had once enjoyed.

The long weeks of cobalt therapy progressed, and Sheri kept in regular contact by phone and letter with her parents. Finally the good news came by phone. "The doctor says the tumor has shrunk and can be safely removed. Mother will have surgery next week," her father announced.

"Thank the Lord!" Sheri responded.

"We have been, dear," her father replied. "He's been very good to us.

"It won't be necessary for you to fly down for the operation this time, Sheri. It should all be quite routine, and since the tumor is smaller, we're not expecting a long recovery."

The evening before the surgery Sheri and Wally telephoned the hospital to have prayer with Mrs. Shaffer. Her spirit was good and she was thrilled that the tumor was smaller and would not require major surgery.

At 9:00 P.M., however, the telephone rang, and Wally answered it.

"Wally!" The voice at the other end of the line was trembling. "The tumor hasn't shrunk. The doctor lied to us," Mr. Shaffer said.

"Dad, that's unethical," Wally exclaimed. "He wouldn't do that. How do you know this to be true?"

"It *is* true. The intern who cared for Mother when she was in the hospital the last time was just in to see her. He had her chart and took another measurement of the tumor. Mother asked him how much the tumor had shrunk, and he said, 'It hasn't shrunk. I have your record. It's the same size as it was when you were in here the last time.' What shall we do, Wally?"

"If that's true, Dad, I sure don't have any faith in your doctor. You should check it out."

"I have. What the intern told us is true. Right now he's concerned that he's going to be in trouble for telling us. I told him not to worry about that. If they did anything to him, I'd cause a ruckus in this hospital they'd never forget. What shall we do about the operation, Wally?"

"I think the final decision must rest with Mother. No one can tell her what to do. It's her leg and it's her life. As tough as it is, she is going to have to decide for herself."

Wally had prayer with his father-in-law, and Mr. Shaffer promised that he would call back to advise them of the decision.

At 9:45 P.M. Mrs. Shaffer telephoned. Wally answered, and Sheri got on the extension phone. "I've decided not to have the operation," Mother explained. "God can heal me if He wants to, and if not, I'd rather die than lose a leg."

"There is always the possibility of an anointing service," her son-in-law said. "If no operation is your decision, you can always appeal your case to God as He outlines in James 5:14."

Mrs. Shaffer did decide to have an anointing service and telephoned Sheri and Wally a few days after her release from the hospital to ask them if they would be present at it.

Sheri and Wally both were on the line as the Shaffers, in a four-way telephone conversation, explained just how they wished the anointing to be conducted.

"I don't want Pastor Dickerson to anoint me," Mrs. Shaffer stated.

"Why not?" Sheri asked.

"I don't like him."

"Has he done something to offend you?"

"No, I just don't like the way he preaches. He's always making appeals. He drives me crazy with his appeals."

Sheri's voice tightened. "But, Mother, that shows he's concerned about his congregation. That's no reason to dislike him."

"He's just concerned about getting more members and more money for the church. That's what *he's* concerned about."

Pastor Dickerson had been instrumental in introducing Wally and Sheri before their marriage, and they knew him well.

"That's not true, Mother," Sheri protested. "I know Pastor Dickerson, and he's a sincere and dedicated man!"

"Well, I don't like him. And I don't want him to anoint me. I don't even want him in the room when I'm anointed. I'm going to ask our former pastor to do it."

The daughter's face felt warm, and as she brushed a lock of hair from her eyes, she noticed her forehead was moist. She couldn't believe what she was hearing. It was the kind of attitude her parents had displayed when she first began praying for their spiritual condition months ago. She had thought that it had changed as the two of them grappled with the cancer problem. But here it was as real as ever.

Apparently Wally sensed his wife's tension, for he broke into the conversation with a low, steady voice. "Mother, anointing is a very sacred service and must be entered into with the proper spiritual preparation. We must remember that there is no power in the oil that is used to anoint someone. The power comes from God, and He can give His power in its fullness only when our attitude is in harmony with His will."

"What you're saying is," the older woman snapped, "I should have Pastor Dickerson anoint me, right?"

"No, you can, of course, have anyone you wish anoint you, but certainly we should have an attitude of peace and unity with one another before entering into such a sacred service."

Mr. Shaffer now broke into the conversation. "I think you've said quite enough, Wally. Mother and I have morning worship together each morning, and we've prayed about this. I don't think we need any sermonizing on the subject."

"I didn't mean to sound like a preacher, Dad. May I just suggest that the two of you read a few chapters from *The Ministry of Healing* before the anointing service?"

"No, you may not. Mother and I have read all we're going to on this subject. Now I think we had best close this conversation. Mother must get to bed. She needs all the rest she can get."

After the awkward goodbyes, Wally and Sheri stood facing each other.

"I'm sorry, honey," he said as he gently took hold of her shoulders.

"Don't be sorry, Wally; you did the best you could." Sheri hugged him tightly and buried her head in his chest as tears began making crooked rivulets down her flushed cheeks.

Three tense days passed, during which Sheri wondered what she should do. Should she write her parents? Should she call Pastor Dickerson? Should she just continue praying? She decided on the latter—at least for now.

The evening of the third day the telephone rang, and when she answered it a familiar voice greeted her.

"Hi, honey," Mrs. Shaffer said. "I want you to know I've been reading *The Ministry of Healing*, as Wally suggested. On pages 228 and 229, in the chapter entitled 'Prayer for the Sick,' I found something that cut straight to my heart. Let me read it to you:

" 'To those who desire prayer for their restoration to health, it should be made plain that . . . in order for them to receive His blessing, sin must be confessed and forsaken. . . . Sin of a private character is to be confessed to Christ. . . . Every open sin should be as openly confessed. Wrong done to a fellow being should be made right with the one who has been offended. If any who are seeking health have been guilty of evilspeaking, . . . these things should be confessed before God and before those who have been offended. . . . When wrongs have been righted, we may present the needs of the sick to the Lord in calm faith, as His Spirit may indicate.'

"I want you to know I've asked Pastor Dickerson to forgive me for my critical attitude toward him, and I've asked him to be present and have a prayer at my anointing."

"Praise God!" Sheri almost shouted the words.

Mrs. Shaffer continued, "I've also read what *The Ministry of Healing* had to say about the relationship of meat eating to cancer in the chapter entitled 'Flesh as Food.' And I've decided I'm not going to eat any more meat. I can see now that without complying with this counsel it would be presumptuous to ask God's healing."

"How does Dad feel about all this?" She held her breath as she waited for a response.

"Your old dad is on the extension, Sheri," Mr. Shaffer broke in. "What Mother said goes for me, too. I guess you're never too old to learn."

The anointing service was held as scheduled, with Sheri and Wally present. Pastor Lundstrom, their former pastor, performed the anointing, but both he and Pastor Dickerson had individual prayers. During the service Mrs. Shaffer said she felt something akin to a shot of electricity go through her leg as the pastors prayed.

The anointing service took place eleven years ago, and Mrs. Shaffer still has her leg. And Sheri and her parents now know that God is great enough to turn something as devastating as cancer into a blessing.

7

Thank God for Debts

Pastor Bill Conklin got out of his car and walked toward the Klooster home. The cool evening air of the Great Smoky Mountains felt refreshing after the hot, humid day he had experienced in the valley.

It was his last visit for the day, and he breathed a prayer as he walked up the fieldstone walkway of the humble home. He had visited here several times within the past two years, hoping to develop a good relationship with Fred Klooster. Fred's wife was a member of his church, and she regularly attended with their two children, Lisa, 12, and Sheila, 8. But the husband had no church affiliation.

Pastor Conklin had succeeded in developing a good relationship with the man. They mutually respected each other, but Fred had never expressed any spiritual interest—that is, until today.

Today he had called the church and left a message with the part-time volunteer secretary that he would like to see Pastor Conklin about putting his daughters in church school. They had made an appointment for 7:30 P.M.

As he approached the door Pastor Conklin glanced at his watch. The digital dial read 7:29. Sheila pushed the screen door open and smiled at him. Her smile revealed two rabbitlike front teeth with an empty space on either side. A dimple in both cheeks, straight blonde hair, and blue eyes brought back memories of his own daughter, now a sophomore in academy.

Cynthia Klooster came from the kitchen. She was a tall, thin woman with delicate features, and her plain face broke easily into a smile. "Come on in, Pastor. I'm real happy you came." As she spoke she dried her hands on her apron. "I'll fetch Fred. Our cow jes' got outta the fence and he had to round her up an' then repair the fence."

"Don't bother him, Cynthia. I'll go outside and see if I can give him a hand."

"Won't hear of it, Pastor. You're all dressed up in your suit. You jes' set down in the big lounge chair while I fetch him."

Bill knew better than to insist on going outside to help Fred. Cynthia was the epitome of Southern hospitality. She and Fred were almost old-fashioned in their respect for a minister. Pastor Conklin always felt like royalty when he visited their home. They didn't have much in material goods, but what they had they shared.

The "lounge chair" Cynthia had referred to was a leather reclining chair left to her when her mother died. The chair looked out of place in the modest room furnished with well-worn furniture of various vintages. But because it was the newest and most comfortable chair in the house, the Kloosters always reserved it for the pastor when he visited. This evening Pastor Conklin appreciated the chair more than usual. It had been a busy day and an extremely hot one. Sitting deep in the chair, he laid his head back. The leather felt cool against his back and arms. How could it have been so hot in the valley today and yet be so cool up here in the mountains tonight? The coolness reminded him that fall was approaching and that in two more weeks school would begin. He still had some homes to visit to see if he could recruit more students for the new eight-grade church school that was opening.

"Pastor, do you like this picture?" Sheila stood next to him, holding a picture of a red lighthouse she had colored from her coloring book. Engrossed in his thoughts, he had almost forgotten that the quiet, even-tempered little girl was in the room.

"Oh, yes, Sheila, I like it very much. You color very nicely, and red is my favorite color."

Her rosebud mouth stretched into a bashful grin. Then she looked down at the floor and a light blush came to her cheeks as she said, "You can have it if you like it, Pastor Conklin."

"Why, thank you, Sheila; I'll put it on my bulletin board at home, right over my desk."

Smiling broadly, the girl then swung around and skipped out the front door without saying another word.

He chuckled to himself as he turned to see her toss her head from side to side as she skipped across the front lawn and out of sight. How uninhibited children are when they feel good about something, he thought.

"Hello there, Preacher!" Fred's welcome was always hardy, and he always called Pastor Conklin "Preacher." Mr. Klooster had entered the house from the rear entrance, through the kitchen, and now stood in the doorway leading from the kitchen to the living room where Conklin sat.

Bill Conklin turned his head to face Fred and then rose to greet him. Fred was of medium height with a wiry body and ruddy complexion. A strong, callused hand reached out for Pastor Conklin's, and the two men shook hands warmly.

Conklin liked the uncomplicated and straightforward man. There was no facade, no game playing in his life. If you asked him a question you got an answer, unless he thought the question was too personal for you to deserve a reply. Then he'd tell you so. "I don't believe in pussyfootin' around," he'd say.

"Sorry I kept you waitin', Preacher. Daisy's jes' gittin' right ornery in her ol' age, and she don't like fences none. She's a good milk cow, though.

"Anyway, you ain't here to listen to mah cow problems. I've got other problems more important. Set down, Preacher."

Fred took a seat on the couch at the end nearest Pastor Conklin's chair, and Cynthia came into the room carrying a tray of lemonade. "Have a glass o' lemonade, Pastor Conklin," she said. "Radio said it was right hot in the valley today."

The minister reached for the lemonade. "It sure was, Cynthia. Feels good to be up here in the mountains tonight." He took a long drink. "That sure tastes good."

"Got plenty more, Pastor Conklin, so you jes' drink all you want."

"Where's Lisa tonight?"

"She's visitin' Grandma Klooster in Gatlinburg [Tennessee] this week," the woman said. "She loves all those little shops up there, an' o' course Grandma spoils her rotten."

Conklin chuckled, then turned to face her husband. "Well, Fred, what's this problem you have on your mind? The message you left at the church was that you were interested in sending your children to the new church school this year."

"That's right, Preacher. I don't like some o' the goin's on at public school. Las' year Lisa was sent a note by a boy that wasn't fit fer a *man* to read, let alone a schoolgirl. I want Lisa and Sheila in a *Christian* school.

"Mah problem is I don't have enough money to send them. You know I work on a dairy farm, an' there ain't but so many hours I can work an' the work is done. It's not like I can work overtime to earn more money.

"I have a house payment, a truck payment, an' by the time I take care of those payments plus the normal bills it takes to run a fam'ly of four, we're jes' plum outta money by the end o' the month. In fact, Preacher, because o' some unexpected house repairs, I'm two months behind now on mah house an' truck payments. I jes' don't see how I can afford another $100 a month to send mah two little girls to church school."

Pastor Conklin leaned forward in his chair. "Fred, this is going to sound about as foolish a thing as you've ever heard, but I'm going to be absolutely honest with you."

"You know that's the way I like it, Preacher." Fred

looked intently at the minister.

"Have you ever considered paying tithe to the Lord?"

"You mean 10 percent of mah income?" Mr. Klooster's eyes grew wide.

"That's right, Fred. Ten percent."

"I know the Good Book talks about that, Preacher, but I don't see how I could ever do that when I can't even make it to the end of the month without runnin' short."

"It doesn't make any sense to me, either, Fred, but it works. You see, God gives us life, physical health, wisdom to get wealth, land to till, water and sun for our crops, and all He asks in return is 10 percent of our income. He gives us 90 percent to do with as we wish. I'd say that was pretty generous of Someone that invests that much in us, don't you think so?"

"Yes, that's a pretty reas'nable request on God's part, but I still don't see how mah income is gonna go further if I have less than I have now to pay mah bills with!"

Bill Conklin reached into his pocket and pulled out his small Bible. "Let me read you something, Fred. It's found in Malachi 3:10. 'Bring ye all the tithes into the storehouse, that there may be meat in mine house.' You see, Fred, the tithe is supposed to be used for the work of God. That's money that really doesn't belong to us. In fact, according to verse 8, God considers it robbery when we use it, because it's God's money. And when we use God's money He can't bless us as He would like to."

Fred listened intently, and Pastor Conklin could hardly believe that after two years of visiting in the home he was finally on a spiritual topic with Mr. Klooster. It seemed to him this was the wrong way to start. After all, they had never discussed salvation, or Jesus' love for sinners, yet here they were talking about tithe. Conklin would never have planned it this way, but he thought, Who am I to question the work of the Holy Spirit?

"How do I know God will bless me if I pay tithe?" Fred asked.

"Let's just read on in this text to get your answer.

'. . . and prove me now herewith, saith the Lord of hosts, if I will not open you the windows of heaven, and pour you out a blessing, that there shall not be room enough to receive it.'

"Fred, there is no surer promise in all the Bible that I could give you. The Lord says, 'Prove Me.' He's challenging you tonight. If you don't believe He'll do it, prove Him. Test Him on this promise."

Mr. Klooster sat silently staring at the Bible text the minister held out in front of him to read. Then slowly he turned and looked into Pastor Conklin's eyes. "Preacher, do you really believe that?"

"I believe it with all my heart, Fred. I've proved God on this many times, and He has never failed me yet."

"OK, Preacher," Fred said in a tone that sounded like an ultimatum was coming, "I want you to set down with me tonight and go over all mah monthly payments. Then compare them with what I earn an' see if I can afford to pay tithe an' still put mah girls in church school."

Fred got up from the couch and disappeared from the room. Cynthia, who was seated in a wooden rocking chair at the other end of the room, looked at Conklin and raised her eyebrows quizzically.

Almost immediately Fred returned with paper and pen in hand and a large envelope under one arm. He pulled the coffee table in front of the couch close to the chair where Conklin was sitting, placed the paper and pen before the pastor, and opened the envelope. The envelope contained bills that needed to be paid.

One by one Fred called out the bills and had the minister write each one in a column on the paper. He asked Cynthia to figure up food and clothing expenses per month and include that amount in the bills column. Then he added the cost of gas and truck maintenance, as well as utilities and house maintenance. Every expense was figured at its absolute minimum. Finally the two men put in tuition and tithe, and Conklin totaled the column and subtracted the amount from Fred's monthly income.

From the figures before them it was plain to see that the Klooster household would be going into debt by $60 every month if they began tithing and sending their children to church school.

"There, Preacher," Mr. Klooster said, "you can see it's impossible for me to pay tithe an' send mah girls to church school."

Pastor Conklin's faith remained undaunted. "Fred, I believe God means what He says. If you begin paying tithe, He will bless you, and you'll be able to send your children to church school." Conklin related some critical financial situations that he and his family had been through and how claiming the Biblical promise had brought them extra money from unexpected sources.

As he spoke, he could see that his personal testimony seemed to move Fred. He also knew that Klooster was a conscientious man, and felt sure the Lord was working on his heart.

The minister paused, then looked straight at Fred. "I'll make a deal with you—if God doesn't keep His word about blessing you if you tithe, I'll quit the ministry."

Klooster's mouth opened wide, and his eyes bulged. "Preacher, are you serious?"

"Yes, I am. If I can't count on the promises of God, then my ministry is worthless."

"OK, here's what I'm gonna do. I'm gonna write out a contract to God. If He keeps His part of the bargain, I'll keep mine." He reached for a sheet of paper and began writing:

"I, Fred Klooster, do hereby make a solemn promise to God to pay my tithe and begin sending my children to church school for two months. Upon completion of the two months, if God has fulfilled His promise to help me keep my children in church school, and if all my other bills are no further behind than now, then I, Fred Klooster, will continue to pay my tithe, and I will become a Christian." Signing the pledge, he handed it to Pastor Conklin.

Placing the pledge on the coffee table before him, the minister asked the Kloosters to join him on their knees in a commitment prayer.

At the close of the prayer Cynthia's face was red and moist with tears, but covered with a full smile. She stepped close to her husband, put her arm around his waist, and squeezed him tightly. He responded by putting his arm around her shoulders and reciprocating.

Fred's face glowed. A serenity rested upon it that made him look years younger—almost boylike. "Thanks, Preacher," he said as he grabbed Conklin's extended right hand in both of his and shook it.

Three weeks passed. Lisa and Sheila had now attended church school for a week. Whenever Pastor Conklin saw Cynthia at church she appeared happy. And when on one occasion he had asked her how things were going, she had responded in a cheery tone, "Jes' *wonderful,* Pastor."

Late on Thursday afternoon of the fourth week Pastor Conklin was in the area of the Klooster home and stopped to see Fred. As he approached the house he could see Mr. Klooster's legs standing next to his Chevrolet truck, his head and chest hidden behind the raised hood.

"Got truck problems, Fred?"

The man straightened up and began wiping his hands on a rag. "I'd shake your hand, Preacher, but as you can see, I'm pretty greasy."

"I've never minded an honest workingman's dirty hand, Fred," the minister replied as he held out his right hand.

The two men shook hands, but Conklin could sense a lack of the usual warmth. "Anything serious?" He nodded toward the truck.

"Don't think so; jes' think it needs some new spark plugs. Don't know how I'm gonna pay for 'em, though."

"What do you mean, Fred? I saw Cynthia last Sabbath, and she implied that your finances were coming along just fine."

"Well, she was prob'ly more optimistic than she should've been." His voice seemed somewhat bitter and tense. "Cynthia's jes' balanced our checkbook, an' we're overdrawn by $30. We've bin countin' every penny an' cuttin' everythin' to bare essentials, an' we're still in the hole. Guess your God jes' ain't comin' through, Preacher."

The abruptness of the words took the minister by surprise, but he managed to maintain his composure. "Fred, sometimes the Lord tests our commitment to see if we've really meant what we've said. The two months aren't up yet. Are you willing to stand by your pledge?"

Staring at the rag in his hands, Klooster began wiping them again. "I'm a man of my word, Preacher. I pledged two months, and two months it will be." Though Fred reaffirmed the pledge, Conklin noted that the man lacked his usual buoyancy.

"God won't let you down, Fred." Pastor Conklin said it as much to strengthen himself as he did for Mr. Klooster's sake, for as he drove home that evening doubt was poking its ugly head into his own heart.

The next day was Friday, and Conklin spent most of it in the church office finalizing his sermon. He had been making notes and studying all week with the thought of presenting a sermon entitled "Be Joyful in the Lord." But as he worked on polishing it, the words seemed a mockery to what he was now experiencing. How could he deliver the sermon tomorrow when his own heart felt troubled?

Had he been presumptuous in saying he would quit the ministry if God didn't come through for Fred? Was he trying to tell God how to deal with His own children? What would he do if God had a plan other than the one he had *thought* the Lord had?

Pastor Conklin had been a minister long enough to know that sometimes a pastor must preach a sermon that he himself needs to hear more than his congregation. This would be one of those sermons, he thought as he gathered up his books and placed them in his briefcase. He closed the case slowly and walked toward the door of his office.

As he reached for the doorknob the telephone rang. He set down his briefcase and went back to the phone on his desk. "Pastor Conklin speaking."

"Pastor Conklin," a breathless voice said on the other end, "this is Cynthia. Jes' *had* to tell ya as soon as I found out. I made a mistake in the figurin' yesterday. We're not $30 overdrawn—we have $20 *left* in our checkbook. An' today I received a check from Fred's mother for $20 to help with the girls' schoolin'. That means we have $40 left until payday, an' payday is Monday. That kind o' money is unheard of in this household for the week before payday!"

That was the beginning of a series of miracles that showered upon the Klooster household. Within the next two weeks Fred had the offer of part-time evening work at a nursery, cultivating and planting trees. And by the time the two-month contract with the Lord had expired, Mr. Klooster not only had kept current with all his bills, but had also caught up on his back payments for the house and truck.

True to his word, Fred gave his heart to the Lord, began taking Bible studies, and eventually was baptized into church membership. By the following summer his enthusiasm for sharing Christ was so strong that the church elected him assistant personal ministries leader.

And a humble family in a humble home nestled in the Great Smoky Mountains has learned they can even thank God for debts.

8

Thank God for Armed Robbery

Manuel Pastor picked up a charred piece of wood that had once been part of the checkout counter of the grocery store. Just why someone had thrown a bomb through its window, no one knew. Perhaps the former owner had made an enemy of someone and this had been a way of getting even. One thing for certain—Manuel was determined it would not happen to him.

Because of the store's condition he had been able to buy the business for a low price. He would remodel it and open a beverage and grocery store like the other four his family already owned in the El Monte, California, area.

His family had begun opening them shortly after arriving in the United States from Panama six years previously, and now the Pastor name was well respected.

Manuel would have no problem getting credit from suppliers. The meat supplier of his family's other stores had already promised to provide him with all he needed under the agreement that Pastor would begin to pay him back with interest as soon as the store was making money.

Since the store was located in the Latino area of El Monte, Manuel felt confident that he would be able to maintain a good relationship with his customers, whose cultural backgrounds he understood. And his shrewd sense of business and personable attitude would undoubtedly bring him the success he desired.

Leaning against the smoke-damaged wall to the left of

the entrance to the store, he lit a cigarette. His mind's eye began to envision the location of the meat case, the meat locker, the beverage cooler, the produce counter, and the shelves of grocery items. Each aisle of groceries will have imported wines on the top shelf, he thought. We Latinos appreciate good wine.

Then he began thinking of his bride of six months. He wanted the store to bring her happiness. It represented the beginning of settling down. Before meeting Yolanda, Manuel had been a heavy gambler. Many friends associated with the racetracks had provided him with tips on horses. Also he enjoyed playing the lottery from Puerto Rico, and he enjoyed card games—the higher the stakes the better. Once he had lost $400 on a single hand in a poker game.

Though he loved gambling and could not imagine ever giving it up completely, he knew he needed some security now that he was married, and he was sure the store would provide it.

Manuel had been told the store was thirty-five by sixty feet. Now, just for fun, he began to pace the width of it. As he reached the approximate halfway point, he noticed to his left a piece of wood almost unmarred by the fire. Stooping down for a closer look, Manuel observed that only one-half inch of a corner of the wood was charred, while the floor surrounding it was completely black. Curious, he lifted the piece of wood to survey it more closely. As he did so, he discovered a Bible beneath it—an English-language Bible totally untouched by the fire. He leafed through the pages—not a mark on them.

Though raised a Catholic, Manuel was not a religious man. But as he gazed at the unharmed Bible in the midst of a charred room, he found himself spiritually moved. Surely God had protected His Book, he thought. It was a Miracle Book. I shall make a special shelf for it on the wall in back of my checkout counter. Perhaps the Miracle Book will bless my business.

He finished the remodeling of the store in late May, and

by early June had stocked it with a large supply of meat, beer, wine, cigarettes, produce, miscellaneous grocery items, and a book rack of pornographic literature.

Almost as soon as Manuel had opened his business he learned that Yolanda was pregnant with their first child. Business was slow, and Manuel became concerned as to how he would support his wife and baby once she had to leave her job. Yolanda worked on the assembly line of an electronics firm, and they lived on her income while the business was getting started. Both of them had determined they would use no money from the business for living expenses. Instead they would put the money back into the business until it became self-sufficient. But now that a baby was on the way, Manuel knew his wife could not continue to work too much longer. Remembering the way God had miraculously saved the Bible from the fire, he thought perhaps the God of the Bible would also help his business get started. Not really knowing how to pray, he simply began to talk to God. "God," he said, "You have to help me, because I'm doing something honest."

Coupled with his talks with God, Manuel began stepping outside his store to ask people to come inside and see what he had. Finally he put some advertising on the radio and invited the disc jockey making the announcements to come to his store for a grand opening. Manuel offered gifts to those who would attend. Since the store's name was Guantanemera, the disc jockey began playing the then-popular Cuban song called "Guantanemera" to advertise the business.

The day of the grand opening many people stopped by to meet the disc jockey, and thus became acquainted with Manuel. His business began to increase and to develop a regular clientele.

At the same time he looked for ways to increase his profit. He started selling black market cigarettes and became involved in some business ventures that pushed the law to the limit. From time to time when advised of a "sure thing," he would gamble. And by December, just six months after the store had opened, Manuel paid the meat supplier in full. Impressed with receiving payment so soon, the man did not charge him any interest.

By spring of the following year, when a little girl, Alexandria Aurilia, was born to the Pastors, it was not necessary for Yolanda to return to work. And within a year and a half after starting the business Manuel had paid off all his debts and now owned six homes, renting five and living in one.

One day a young Cuban woman came to the store, accompanied by her 5-year-old daughter. The woman's fine features and gentle spirit attracted his attention. She purchased several items and, after paying her bill, struggled with her two grocery bags. Discovering that she had no one to help her and had no car, Manuel arranged to have her purchases delivered to her home. Thereafter, each time Mrs. Hernandez came to shop, Manuel had the food brought to her.

About two months after he had met Mrs. Hernandez, a black limousine with Chicago area license plates pulled in front of Guantanemera, and a tall, dark-haired man dressed in a sharkskin suit entered the store.

Manuel had been showing a new employee how to arrange the various brands of beer on the last aisle of shelves to the right of the store as the man drove up. He pretended he hadn't seen the stranger enter the store.

The man stood at the end of the aisle where Pastor was working with the new employee and called out, "Manuel."

Approaching him, Pastor asked suspiciously, "How do you know my name?"

The man smiled broadly, revealing a near-perfect set of white teeth. "Oh, I know you. I also know that although you are well liked and respected in this neighborhood, you also have a good business head and are nobody's fool."

Manuel's brow creased and his stocky frame tensed. "How do you know so much about me?"

Apparently seeking to relax the tension, the man said, "Thank you for helping my wife."

"Your wife?"

"Yes. My wife speaks very highly of you. I'm Mr. Hernandez."

Manuel reached out his hand to Mr. Hernandez, but faltered slightly as he spoke. "Well, I'm happy to meet you. But I must admit I'm a bit surprised. I had assumed Mrs. Hernandez was either a widow or divorced, for she never mentioned her husband."

"My wife is not a talker. We don't like a lot of people knowing too much about us. But as I mentioned before, I know quite a bit about you."

By now Manuel was beginning to feel some apprehension as to why Hernandez had dropped in to see him and just who he might be. "What else do you know about me?"

"I know you like to gamble and that you enjoy making money." Hernandez glanced toward the new employee and then gestured for Pastor to follow him. The man walked past two aisles of groceries to the checkout counter and then lowered his voice. "I'm involved in a very lucrative business, Manuel. And when I benefit financially I like to share my good fortune with people I can trust. I know what kind of person you are, and I'd like you to become involved in my business." Then he proceeded to tell Pastor how he could steal from millionaires by using their credit card numbers to make purchases.

Manuel had no desire to get into something so big and so illegal, but he was afraid to say that he wanted no part of it lest he offend the man and make an enemy, so he said, "I like your idea, it's very interesting, but it's going to be impossible for me to get involved right now because I'm so busy with this business. Maybe some time in the future we can work together."

Pastor's answer seemed to satisfy Hernandez, and after encouraging him not to wait too long, he left the store.

One week later a man from Tijuana solicited his help in supervising a drug connection that involved a suitcase full of money. Once again Manuel hedged by saying, "I can't help you right now because, you know, I have this business and I'm so busy. Maybe someday I can help you, but not now."

As others approached him about more ventures, Manuel began to fear for his life and repeatedly had the feeling that someone was going to kill him.

On a beautiful Sunday morning in May, Manuel found it hard to go to work. The warm sun, the blue sky, and the frothy white clouds seemed to beckon him to take his family on a picnic. Alexandria was now 2 years old, and another baby was on the way. He looked forward to locating a new home for his family, as Yolanda was becoming concerned with the neighborhood in which they lived. Within the past few months they had witnessed gunshots being fired from a car. On another occasion a man was killed when he tried to rob the bar located on the corner of their street. Today Manuel longed to take his family to the country for a reprieve from the pressures of city living. But, of course, he had the business to care for.

But he consoled himself with the idea that Sundays were shorter. He would be out of the store by 2:00 P.M., and then they could take a drive in the country and perhaps get a frozen custard. Alexandria will love that, he thought.

Manuel thought about his daughter and about *The Bible Story* set he had ordered the week before from a book salesman who had stopped by Guantanemera. When the girl was a little older she would enjoy seeing the pictures and listening to the stories in them. The books would be arriving in another week.

Entering the store, Manuel turned the lights on and knelt to straighten the magazines and books in the rack located to the left of the front door. Then he heard some movement within the store. Turning his head, he found himself staring at the legs of a man standing over him. Lifting his eyes to see the man's face, Manuel discovered a handgun pointed at him. In his mid to late 20s, the gunman was of medium build and about five feet ten inches in height. He had light hair with a tinge of red in it and a full, but neatly trimmed, beard. In back and to the left of the first man was a second, smaller individual, clean shaven with dark hair.

The man holding the gun said, "Get up," and then cocked the weapon as Manuel rose to his feet. The other man went to the cash register and removed the money in it. Pastor watched, and as he did his eye caught sight of a picture of Alexandria that he had hung on the wall immediately in back of the checkout counter. "O Lord," he prayed silently, "I want to raise my children. Don't let them kill me. I promise You, I will give You my heart, my children, my family, and I will live for You. I will prove to You that I love You, but don't let them kill me."

After the second man had taken the money, the man with the gun ordered, "OK, now walk until I tell you to stop." His voice cracked as he spoke, and it trembled slightly. He's nervous, Manuel thought. It wouldn't take much for him to pull that trigger.

Manuel headed toward the back of the store, and the robber followed him, past the twenty-eight-foot meat case and the door to the meat locker. At the rear of the store the man told Pastor to turn right. As Manuel approached the milk and soft drink cooler, the man said, "Lie down."

Surely he will kill me now, Manuel told himself as he lay on the floor with his cheek pressing against the tile and his head turned so he could see the gunman. Silently he continued to pray for the Lord to spare his life.

The gunman backed away from him down the center aisle of the store and disappeared out the front door.

Manuel couldn't believe his eyes. The men had left without killing him. "Thank You, Lord," he prayed as he scrambled to his feet and hurried to lock the door. Quickly he telephoned the police, then knelt down in the middle of his store and prayed: "Lord, thank You for saving my life. I will keep my promise to You. I give You my heart, my children, my family. Show me what I can do for You to repay You for saving my life."

The police arrived, and Manuel gave them descriptions of the two men, but they were never apprehended. Manuel closed the store somewhat early that day, but did not tell his wife what had happened.

Each morning of the following week as Manuel entered his store he knelt down to pray. His prayer was always the same: "Lord, I want to keep my promise to You. Send me someone to show me Your true message. I want to raise my children to serve You, and I want You to use me. You must have a purpose for me since You have saved my life."

On the following Saturday at twelve-thirty in the afternoon a Latino man came to his store dressed in a black suit, white shirt, and black tie. As Pastor saw the man he became excited. What a nice shining face he has, Manuel thought. The man was carrying a Bible, and as he approached, something told Manuel that here was the "someone" with the "true message" he had been praying for all week. So certain was he that he nodded toward the Bible in the man's hand and asked, "Is this for me?"

"Yes," the man said, and handed him the Bible.

"Is it in Spanish?"

"Yes."

"OK," Manuel replied, "I have something for you in English." Pastor turned and reached for the English Bible that had survived the fire and handed it to the man.

The man accepted the Bible and then introduced himself as Leonard Santana. "Are you interested in knowing more about the Bible?" he asked.

"Yes, I want to understand it."

"Why don't you come to my church with me this Wednesday evening?"

Manuel responded by handing Leonard a business card and saying, "We will see. Call me on Wednesday."

On Monday Pastor received the shipment of *The Bible Story* set he had ordered. As he read the books himself he began to cry and said aloud, "Now I have met the great God I have been praying to each morning, the God who saved my life."

Keeping the books at his store, Manuel read whenever he had a few moments. Going through the Creation story, he learned that the Sabbath is the seventh day. Why, he thought, do all the churches have services on Sunday, the *first* day?

On Wednesday afternoon Santana telephoned him. "Manuel, remember, today is the day we made arrangements to go to church together."

"Oh, I'm so busy." But immediately after saying those words he remembered his promise to God. This may be the message from the Lord I have been praying about, he told himself. I can't refuse to go, I have promised Him I will follow where He leads me. Quickly Manuel added, "Listen, it's OK. You come to my store tonight, and I will follow you to church."

Normally Manuel closed the store at 8:00 P.M., but this night he locked it a little before seven and followed Leonard in his car as the man led the way to the midweek prayer service.

They parked their cars in back of the church and entered it from the rear. The program was already in progress. As Manuel walked into the rear of the sanctuary he noticed there were no images of saints in the church, and he felt uncomfortable. It was strange to be inside a church without statues of saints. Yet I have prayed that God would lead me to the true message, he reminded himself, and I must keep my promise to Him.

The two men sat down in the back of the sanctuary just as the pastor invited those in attendance to kneel for prayer. Manuel and Leonard knelt also. As people began to pray, Pastor heard many of the worshipers mention him in their prayers. Some had seen him enter with Santana, and they prayed, "Thank You, Lord, for bringing the store man to our church." Others prayed, "Please bless the man from the grocery business and bless his family."

Manuel's heart raced. How do these people know me? he wondered. Then he silently talked to God, "Lord, how nice these people are to pray for me and my family."

When prayer ended he began studying the others. I know that man, Manuel thought to himself. That's the man who sold me *The Bible Story* books. And that lady over there is a customer of mine. And that woman comes to my store too. And that man . . . and that woman.

After prayer meeting closed, Pastor and Santana walked outside into the parking lot, but the church members followed them and approached Manuel. They shook his hand, and some hugged him. How friendly and loving these people are, he thought.

One thin woman greeted Manuel and said, "It's wonderful to have you here tonight. Won't you come and worship with us on Sabbath?"

Because Manuel had read the story of Creation in *The Bible Story* books, he knew that when she mentioned the word "Sabbath" she meant the seventh day—Saturday. And he thought, Here is a church that keeps the real Sabbath of the Bible. Once again he felt the Lord was leading, but for some reason he felt annoyed at her request. After all, what did this woman expect him to do, close his store and start attending church on Saturday *this week*?

He looked at a building adjacent to the church and noticed it had an outside stairway leading from the ground floor to the second floor. Pointing to the stairway, he said, "Do you see that stairway?" His voice was brusk as he continued, "You wouldn't expect me to jump from the bottom of those stairs to the top in one bound, would you?"

Her face blushed lightly and she looked down at the ground.

Quickly Manuel got into his car and drove away. But then his conscience began to bother him. He knew he had hurt the woman's feelings, and he felt sorry for the way he had responded to her.

When he reached home he told his wife that he had gone to church.

"What kind of church?" she asked.

"I don't know. I only know that the people there are nice. They prayed for me and they prayed for you."

On Friday Leonard stopped by the store and invited him to attend church with him the next day. At the suggestion Pastor became angry. "Go away. Do you want me to lose my business? Don't you know that Saturday is the best business day for me?" With that Manuel took hold of Leonard's arm and walked him briskly to the door. Once at the door, Manuel pushed him out his store as he said, "Go away and leave me alone!"

All the while Leonard had remained silent, and now Manuel watched as the man walked slowly away from the store with his head bowed. Manuel tried to concentrate on his work the rest of the afternoon, but his mind kept straying to Santana and the way he had treated him.

That evening Pastor took some of *The Bible Story* books to his home to read. While waiting for his wife to finish preparing supper, he leafed through the volumes. As he scanned a page his eyes fell on the words " 'Six days shalt thou labour, and do all thy work: but the seventh day is the sabbath of the Lord thy God.' "

The next morning Manuel went to his store, but he found it impossible to concentrate on his work. Finally he walked behind his meat case, unrolled the white paper that he used to wrap meat, and cut a long piece of it off with a knife. Then he took a black felt-tip pen and wrote on the paper, "Closed Saturday Because It Is the Day of the Lord." He stuck the sign on the front door and went to church.

This time Manuel paid close attention as he drove past the front of the church, and he noticed a sign identifying it as the Seventh-day Adventist Church. As he entered, the members greeted him heartily, some with hugs, some with thanksgiving. And Manuel began to recognize more of his customers.

He saw an elderly woman whom he recognized as Gollita Calderon. She had long white hair wrapped into a bun at the back of her head. Later he discovered that she was the wife of the book salesman—or what the church members called a literature evangelist—who had sold him *The Bible Story* set. After the church service, she and her husband, Felipe, invited him to their home for Sabbath dinner.

The next Sabbath Manuel again went to church and brought his wife and daughter with him. This time he saw two men that he recognized as men who had written him bad checks when they had shopped in his store on a few occasions. The fact that they attended the church discouraged him. But as he sat there he began thinking, Well, no one is perfect. Then he breathed a prayer, "God, let me forget about these men. Let me forgive and forget the past."

That Sabbath Manuel met more people he knew, and it excited him. He knew them as good people, and more and more he began to relate to the faith they represented.

As Pastor stepped from the church that day, he saw some members leaving the building adjacent to it. He noticed that they were handing clothes and food to some people. "What is that all about?" he asked someone.

"Oh, we have a program to help people in need. That is our Community Services building. In it we keep clothes and food for those who need help."

Manuel went into the building and saw for himself the stock of food and rows of clothing. Although he left without saying a word, he thought to himself, These are people that care about poor people, and they care about me, too.

Wednesday evening, when he arrived at prayer meeting, he had filled his station wagon with hundred-pound bags of food for the Community Services center.

All that Manuel saw caused him to love the people of the church, and his continued study of the Bible made him realize more and more that they were truly trying to follow what the Bible teaches.

Examining his own life, he began to pray, "Lord, You will have to do something with me; I need to make some changes."

As Manuel continued studying *The Bible Story* and checking the stories with the Bible he had received from Leonard, he realized that the Holy Spirit wanted to live in his body. He decided that he must stop drinking alcoholic beverages and quit smoking. As he gave the habits up, he came under conviction that if it was bad for his health, it was also wrong for him to provide such things for other people. So he threw out all the cigarettes he had been selling and stopped buying any more of them on the black market. Next he called the companies that supplied him with beer and wine and told them to come pick up the stock in his store. Before he could telephone one beer company, however, the truck arrived with the weekly supply. Manuel greeted the truck driver by saying, "I don't want any more beer."

The man looked astonished and said, "Are you crazy? You know you make a lot of money with this brand of beer."

"I know, but I don't want any more."

After studying the eleventh chapter of Leviticus, Manuel next removed all the unclean meat he had in his store. Within one month after his decision to keep the Sabbath his store was empty of anything he felt he could not conscientiously sell.

Soon customers began to complain. Some thought he was crazy. Some wrote nasty letters and placed them under his door. Some called him names, and others spit at him as he walked down the street. Still others asked him questions about his new faith. Pastors of other denominations who had been his customers tried to dissuade him from his new religion, but instead he appealed to them to accept what the Bible says and pleaded with them to put the truths of the Bible into practice.

Even Manuel's family members who owned the other grocery stores began to turn against him. They told him that he was foolish and that he was causing his wife and child to suffer because of his foolishness.

Fortunately, Yolanda had grown to love the truths from the Bible she had studied with her husband, and she supported him in his decision to please the Lord.

One evening as they knelt together for prayer they both began to cry as they prayed, "Lord, the business is down.

THANK GOD FOR ARMED ROBBERY

You know our customers, family, and friends all think we are fools. What can we do?" As they prayed they both felt impressed that the Lord desired them to sell the business.

The following Sunday as he went to open the door to his store, he found two men waiting for him. One man, Daniel, was the milkman who supplied his store twice a week. The other was Luis, a Cuban customer of his. "What has been happening to you, Manuel?" Luis asked. "You look so despondent."

"Oh, I want to throw away this business; I don't want it any more," Pastor replied. "I would sell it for whatever anybody would give me for it."

"I'll give you $10,000," Luis said.

Though Manuel's business was worth many times that amount, Manuel replied, "Give me the $10,000 and it's yours."

The Cuban's eyes grew wide. "I was kidding you, Manuel, but if you're serious, I'll give you $10,000 for it."

"I'm serious."

"OK, by Friday I'll have the $10,000. You can consider the business sold as of right now."

The next Sabbath the Pastors were planning to attend their first camp meeting. Manuel praised the Lord that he would be able to go without the weight of the business upon him.

But when Friday arrived, Luis came to the store and said, "I'm sorry, Manuel, I couldn't get the money." His eyes filled with tears as he continued, "I'm still trying. I know this is the chance of a lifetime for me."

The Lord has another plan, Manuel thought as he closed his business that Friday afternoon.

At camp meeting the next day the number of people in attendance—more than three thousand—amazed the Pastors. At the close of the morning worship service Manuel's pastor, Victor Collins, an Argentinian, approached Manuel and asked him to give his personal testimony during the afternoon service about how he had found Christ as his Saviour. Manuel was apprehensive about speaking before such a large audience, but when Pastor Collins assured him that it might inspire others at the meeting to commit their lives to Christ, he agreed.

After Manuel had presented his testimony, many Latino people came to him and wept with him and encouraged him to hold fast to the Lord, for surely God had another plan for the sale of his store.

As the people pressed around him, he noticed someone standing on the edge of the crowd. The man's eyes were red and his face was wet with tears. That's one of the men that use to write me bad checks, Manuel thought. Pastor Collins' words came quickly to his mind: "Your testimony may inspire others at this meeting to commit their lives to Christ." Later Manuel learned that it was in fact what had happened. Manuel's story had reached his heart.

When Manuel had finished speaking with the crowd of people, Pastor Collins said, "Manuel, I will be having a baptism next Sabbath in church. I would like to baptize you."

"OK, but pray for me because I want to sell my business. I want to be baptized, and I don't believe either the contacts or the environment of that store are good for me any longer."

Wednesday, Manuel went to prayer meeting, and there he made a commitment to God. "Lord, if I don't sell the business by Friday, I'm going to cut off the liquor license and close it."

On Friday morning the business had not sold, so he went to the liquor license bureau to have the license canceled. The clerk behind the counter said, "You are crazy to cut off this liquor license. This is where the money is in a store like yours."

"I don't want to sell any more liquor."

"Why don't you sell the license to somebody else then? At least you'll make some money out of the deal. But to just cancel it is absolutely crazy!"

Manuel's face flushed. "Listen," he said, "Christian people do not sell this type of merchandise. I am a

Seventh-day Adventist, and I have to respect God's Bible."

The clerk looked at him in disgust, shook his head, and said, "You're crazy." He continued to mutter under his breath as he prepared the necessary forms.

As Manuel climbed into the plush seat of his new Caprice and started the car, the padded dash and the stereo music seemed to mock the sense of loss he was experiencing. As he pulled into traffic, he could feel his eyes burning. Soon hot tears made slow streams down his cheeks. "Lord," he prayed, "I *am* crazy, but I'm happy with You and my family. My conscience is now free. I feel clean; I feel right with You. That's worth all the money in the world."

Parking his car, he walked to the front door of his store. As he put the key into the lock he felt the press of a hand on his shoulder. At the same time a man's voice said, "Manuel."

Pastor turned and looked into the face of Daniel, his milk deliveryman. "Manuel, if you don't sell the business to the Cuban for $10,000, I'll give you $5,000 more."

Pastor searched his face. "What did you say?"

"Don't sell the business to the Cuban. I'll give you $5,000 more, and I'm prepared to take the store today."

Manuel's face turned pale. "Daniel, I just came from the liquor license bureau. I've cut off the liquor license."

Without flincing a muscle, Daniel said, "I don't care; I want the business. I'll give you $10,000 cash today and the other $5,000 in installments of $500 a week."

Bowing his head, Pastor reached for the handkerchief in his back pocket. "Lord," he said silently, "You have answered my prayer."

That day Manuel arranged the transaction with Daniel and gave him the key to the store. The next day Manuel was baptized. Sometime later Yolanda was also baptized. Within six months he began working as a literature evangelist selling Christian books to families in his own neighborhood. He saw some of his former customers won to the Lord and one entire family baptized.

Today Manuel is the associate publishing director for the

Hispanic work in the Illinois Conference of Seventh-day Adventists. In seven years he led his literature evangelists to sell more than $2 million worth of Spanish literature and increase their sales from $100,000 to $500,000 per year. His literature evangelists are also responsible for beginning and building a new church in the heart of Chicago.

It's amazing what the Lord can produce from an armed robbery, isn't it?

9

Thank God for Cystic Fibrosis

Josie lay on her back, head down on a slanted board placed on top of her hospital bed. The clap of the nurse's cupped hands on her 6-year-old chest sounded hard, even cruel, and Ellie's eyes grew wide as she watched the procedure. So this is the postural drainage I've heard about, the woman thought.

"OK, Josie, now cough it up," the nurse said.

The girl took a deep, raspy breath, coughed, and then spit into a paper cup the nurse held to her mouth. Then they repeated the same process.

Josie, a victim of cystic fibrosis, laughed at the vibration of her voice as she tried to talk to the nurse while being clapped. Her relaxed attitude put Ellie at ease, and soon the volunteer aid was watching the treatment with marked interest.

Ellie had become acquainted with Josie and the other children at the United Way health-care center three weeks earlier when she had begun donating her time as a "play lady." The center housed children born with various incurable maladies who came from homes that were financially, intellectually, or morally unable to care for them.

Some of the children had loving homes and were able to return on weekends to a normal family environment. Others, like Josie, could go home only on rare occasions and for only short periods of time because they could not be assured proper care at home. Ellie had put together bits and pieces of information about Josie that she had heard from the staff, volunteers, and visitors. She had learned that on five different occasions the health-care center had tried to reinstate Josie with her mother and stepfather, but each time the story had been the same. Josie had returned to the center with pneumonia. Failure to administer the postural drainage procedure routinely caused mucus to build up in the child's lungs, and pneumonia had been the inevitable result. Her lungs were now so scarred that the health-care center could not risk another attempt to keep her in her home environment. And so she would spend the rest of her life in the facility.

As Josie climbed down from the slanted board and joined the other children who were playing table games, Ellie cornered the nurse. "Mrs. Chandler, how long do cystic fibrosis children live?"

The woman's bright-blue eyes clouded as she heard the question. "Well, Miss Ellie [a name the children had coined for Ellie], that depends a lot on the kind of care they're given. Some have lived to their early 30s; most live to their teens. Josie will be lucky to make it to 9 or 10. A common cold could prove fatal to her."

Ellie's body tensed. Nine or 10 . . . a common cold . . . The words echoed through her mind as she stood staring at the child who was deeply engrossed in play with the other children.

Some childish prank at the table suddenly caused the children to laugh. Josie threw back her head in glee, her thick dark-brown hair glistening in a late-afternoon sunbeam. She seems so happy, Ellie thought. Yet I'm watching someone who is slowly dying, and there is nothing I can do to prevent it.

That night Josie's dark eyes and impish face remained in her mind as she drove to her parents' home, where she lived. "Oh, God," she prayed, "what a world we live in. So far different from Your original plan for us. You gave us life, and Satan has brought us death. It seems so unfair that little children must suffer because of a sin of Adam, and yet I know that is 'the wages of sin' that the Bible speaks of. Genetic deterioration began with sin, and it continues to erode us. Miracle of miracles that the human race hasn't become extinct long before now.

"I would love to see Josie in the new earth, Lord," Ellie continued. "I'd love to hear her laugh without the pale of death surrounding her. I'd love to hear her breathe without the raspy sound. And I'd love to see her distended chest the size of a normal child's. I know You would love to see that too, Lord, otherwise that desire wouldn't be in my own heart."

As Ellie continued volunteering at the center, she learned a great deal from the children. Having formerly been a volunteer at an orphanage for normal children, Ellie saw a marked difference in the behavior of these children. Rarely did she observe them whining or complaining. They took their medicine, shots, inhalants, and treatments all without a whimper. What's more, they seemed to sense their need and support for one another, and often spoke words of encouragement to each other.

Once when "Little Linda" ("little" to differentiate her from another older Linda) was anticipating a new treatment, another child said, "Oh, it's not so bad, Little Linda; I've had that treatment before." Then a small arm slipped around the girl to assure her everything would be all right.

And toys and games were common property. If someone received a new game for a birthday, part of the joy was being able to share it with friends. Often Ellie observed the children with wonder as they let each other play with their things. It reminded her of the Biblical text of Acts 4:32 about the attitude of the early Christian church: "Neither said any of them that ought of the things which he possessed was his own; but they had all things common."

These children, despite their afflictions, have something that normal children know nothing about, Ellie thought to herself.

On a sunny day in August, two months after Ellie had

begun helping at the center, she once again entered the health-care center. The children swarmed her as usual for their welcome hugs and kisses, and she stooped down to receive all the embraces. After she had greeted each child, Little Linda spoke up. "Johnny went home to heaven last night, Miss Ellie." The girl's voice was calm and low, reflecting neither sadness nor joy—just the stark reality of what had happened.

"He was having trouble breathing last night, so they took him to the big hospital," Josie added.

The "big" hospital was City Hospital. The children's health-care center was not equipped for sophisticated treatment, and when an emergency arose or the children required special therapy, the center took them to City Hospital.

A chill passed through the woman as she heard the words the children spoke. It was the first time a child had died since she had begun volunteering at the center. She wanted to say, "Oh, no! It can't be!" But the ten children that crowded around her didn't look at death the same way she did. Death was an ever-present reality they lived with daily. Seeing one of their friends "go home to heaven" wasn't something they feared—it was something they expected.

In October the health center planned a large Halloween party. The week before the party the children talked to Ellie about what costumes they planned to wear.

"I'm going to be a clown," Stephanie said. Ellie took the mask from the girl's red scaly hands and looked into her bespectacled crossed eyes. The disease that wracked Stephanie's body covered the surface of her skin from head to toe. A nurse had once told Ellie what the disease was called, but she couldn't remember. All she knew was that it had been hard for her to feel comfortable touching Stephanie when she first got acquainted with her. But now her arm slipped easily around the redheaded girl's waist, and she squeezed her tightly.

Ellie held the smiling clown face in front of Stephanie's.

"I'll bet you'll get the prize for the funniest costume," she laughed, hugging the child.

"I'm going to be a hobo," Little Linda told her.

"And I'm going to be a princess," Josie added. "Are you going to come to our party, Miss Ellie?"

"I don't know, Josie."

The girl frowned. "Oh, Miss Ellie, please come. I *want* you to be there."

Soon the other children followed her lead, as they so often did. Though younger than most of the children in Ellie's area, Josie was a natural leader. She of all of them seemed to manifest characteristics of self-will. In fact, Josie was the only child that showed an attitude of selfishness on occasion. Ellie observed it sometimes when the girl would be coloring with someone else. She would choose the best picture for herself. Or if the children were playing games, Josie would be first in selecting the color she wished.

As Ellie grew to love the children more and more, she began to plan activities for them. Once she gathered neighbors, friends, and hospital staff together and put on a play for the children, complete with music, costumes, props, and Walt Disney characters come-to-life. The play portrayed the advantages of living life in harmony with faith, hope, and charity. It culminated with a sing-along of the children's favorite songs.

Being about the same size and coloring as Julie Andrews, who played Mary Poppins in the Walt Disney movie by the same name, Ellie dressed like the character for the day. She had a part in the play and then led the children in singing songs such as "A Spoonful of Sugar" and "Super-cali-fragil-istic-expi-ali-docious." The program and her part in it endeared the children to her more than ever. Because of their love for her the Bible stories she would tell them on occasion began to mean more and more to the children. Sometimes she would stay with them until bedtime, pray with them, and then tuck them in for the night.

One day when Ellie came to visit, she noticed Josie was

exceptionally radiant. She couldn't wait until the woman had greeted the other children, and shouted above their chattering, "Miss Ellie, I got a new dress from my mommy!"

The woman's mind raced. Could it be that the child's mother was beginning to show some interest in her daughter? I've never once seen her visit, Ellie thought, yet obviously she must have come if she's brought the girl a dress. Oh, how wonderful for Josie—no wonder she's so thrilled.

Josie's eyes were round as silver dollars as she continued, "And she brought me a pair of new shoes, too!" Then her excitement triggered her chronic cough.

"Josie, calm down a little."

Ignoring the statement, she continued talking. "Oh, Miss Ellie, you've got to see my dress. It has lace on it and tiny pink flowers and everything!" Josie began to cough again, but took the woman by the hand and pulled her to the small wardrobe beside her bed.

Ellie had never seen Josie in a dress, except at the Halloween party when she had worn the princess costume. Slacks and a T-shirt were the norm for her. Seeing how thrilled the girl was at the thought of owning a new dress suddenly cut through the fog of her mind. Perhaps it is the first dress she's ever had. If not the first, it must be very close to it. I've never seen a child so excited about a new dress, Ellie thought.

Quickly Josie opened the wardrobe door and grabbed the hanger holding the precious dress. Her face beamed as she held the dress out to her adult friend.

Ellie took the royal garment and then felt her stomach tighten. The "new" dress looked like a secondhand reject. The pink flowers were set in a background of yellowed white, and the dingy gray lace hung detached from the garment in several places. She hoped that the girl couldn't detect her disappointment. But Josie's excitement was enough for both of them. Giving Ellie some precious time to sort through her emotions, she returned to the wardrobe and took out her "new" shoes.

"And lookit my new shoes!" she squealed, handing Ellie a dirty pair of once-white tennis shoes.

Anger, resentment, and bitterness all welled up within Ellie. The mother only has one other child, she thought. The husband is working, and yet *this* is the best she can bring this little girl?

All the bits Ellie had heard about Josie's mother that she had tried to ignore as hearsay suddenly seemed all too real. Statements made by volunteers and visitors echoed through her mind: "Josie's mother? Oh, I know her. She has quite a way with the men . . . " " . . . a woman who's more concerned with carousing than caring for children." "If Josie had received proper care at home she wouldn't have had pneumonia six times in her short 6 years."

Ellie's mind raced as she stood holding the tattered dress in one hand and the well-worn tennis shoes in the other. Suddenly she became aware of a bright-eyed little face staring up at her, waiting for a comment.

What can I say? Ellie thought. I can't say the dress is beautiful. And I can't say what I really feel.

Finally she fell to her knees, and the tattered dress and the well-worn tennis shoes crisscrossed behind Josie as Ellie enveloped her in a bear hug. "I'm so happy for you, Josie." She fought back tears as she pressed the child tightly to her breast.

That evening Ellie moved mechanically through her playtime with the children and left a little earlier than usual. On her way out she stopped at the supervisor's office.

"Good evening, Mrs. Shepherd. May I speak with you for a moment?" Ellie asked as she stood in the doorway.

"Why, of course you may." The supervisor was a large woman in her early 50s with a round face and ruddy complexion. Love seemed to radiate from her, and it seemed to Ellie that her heart was big enough to love all the world's hurting children.

"Mrs. Shepherd," Ellie said as she entered the office, "would it be all right if I bought some clothes for Josie? I mean, she wouldn't have to know who gave them to her. I would be happy just to give them to you for you to pass along to her. You could tell her they were donated to the center, or whatever you'd wish."

The older woman's whole face smiled when she said, "You must have seen the dress and the tennis shoes."

Ellie's eyes blazed as she blurted out, "How can any mother be so thoughtless and cruel?"

Mrs. Shepherd grew serious, and she revealed a dimension of herself that Ellie had not seen before. "Some mothers just don't recognize a gift from God when they have received one, Ellie. Josie's mother will have many regrets to live with one day, but right now she doesn't see or realize where her path is leading her. Nor is it our job here at the center to reform her. It *is*, however, our job to provide tender, loving care to those who are hurting.

"Your offer is a kind and generous one. The center will be pleased to receive any donation of clothes you would be willing to give."

After waiting a couple weeks until the newness of the tattered dress had passed, Ellie purchased a mint-green dress for Josie. It had a lace-surrounded inset beneath the collar on the front of it. The inset contained delicate pink embroidered flowers.

Josie never knew who had given her the dress, but when she showed it to "Miss Ellie," the woman was able to say honestly, "It's beautiful, Josie."

After that, Ellie kept a watch on Josie's clothes. When anything appeared worn, she would buy a replacement and give it to Mrs. Shepherd.

A year and a half of volunteering at the center passed quickly, and soon it was nearly Christmas.

The children were enjoying the Christmas tree and decorations of the season. Many talked of going home for the holidays. To her surprise, Josie announced, "I'm going home for Christmas too, Miss Ellie."

The woman checked with one of the nurses to find out if what the child was saying was true or just the optimistic exaggeration of a child. The nurse assured Ellie that it was true. Josie's mother had been in to visit the day before and had made arrangements to have her home for a few hours on Christmas Day.

After talking to the nurse, Ellie went to the table where five of the children were playing. Three were playing a game and two, Josie and Stephanie, were coloring. Josie had just turned to a new page in the Christmas coloring book, and Ellie heard her say flippantly, "Look at the Baby Jesus in the manger."

The child's words had a strange tone to them, almost a mocking one. Josie was manifesting her occasional haughty spirit, but this time it had made light of something sacred, and that caught Ellie's full attention.

Ellie tried to put things back into perspective by interjecting softly, "Baby Jesus came into this world to die for us so that we could live in heaven forever, Josie."

The child gave a disgusted glance toward the ceiling, rolled her eyes, and then said in the same haughty tone, "Oh, God."

It shocked Ellie. None of the children had ever used the Lord's name in such a careless manner. Where in the world has she picked up this phrase? she wondered. Keeping her voice firm but low, she said, "Josie, don't use God's name in that manner."

Josie laughed and then repeated the words again.

Ellie had never seen Josie defiant of authority before, and she didn't like what she was observing. It was easy for her to blame the words and their tone on the child's mother. With the prospect of going home in a few days, she thought, was Josie trying to imitate her mother's mannerisms?

Once again Ellie tried to impress the girl with the seriousness of her behavior. "Josie, we must never use God's name in that manner. God calls it taking His name in vain."

Again she said the phrase.

Becoming concerned with Josie's attitude, Ellie found

herself quickly responding, "Josie, if you use God's name like that once more, I'm going to spank you." She surprised herself with her reaction, having never spanked any of the children before. For that matter, being single and not having children of her own, she had never spanked *any* child. What would she do if Josie decided to test her?

Ellie didn't have long to ponder. Josie quickly put her to the test.

What in the world shall I do now? Ellie thought. How can I spank a child who has only a short time to live? Yet if I don't follow through with my threat, she'll think me inconsistent. And what will I be telling her about my God? That she can break His commands without receiving the results?

She made her decision. Without any display of anger, Ellie rose from her seat and gave the child two quick spanks on the buttocks. Josie didn't cry; she just looked surprised. The slaps weren't as hard as the claps Josie regularly received during the postural drainage procedure, but they proved significant.

After the spanking Ellie turned back toward the table where the other children had been playing. "How is that game coming along?" she asked as if nothing had happened.

Soon she and the children were involved in the game.

In a few moments Ellie noticed, out of the corner of her eye, that Josie was standing close to her side. Then she saw her slip into the chair next to Stephanie, who was still coloring. "May I color with you, Stephanie?"

Stephanie's red blemished face creased into a broad grin. "Sure, Josie. Let's each start a new picture. I've got this one almost finished."

"You choose the picture you want to color, Stephanie. I'll color whichever picture you don't want."

Quickly Ellie responded, "That's a very unselfish gesture, Josie. I'm proud of you."

The girl looked at her and smiled sheepishly.

That night Ellie stayed to tuck the children in bed. But

she saved her goodnight to Josie until last.

She and the girl knelt by the side of the hospital bed and Ellie waited as Josie prayed, "Dear Jesus, thank You for coming into the world so that we could live with You forever in heaven. And thank you for Miss Ellie. Bless my mommy and little brother and Stephanie and all my other friends. Amen."

Then Ellie prayed, "Thank You, Lord, for Josie. And thank You for making her so kind and courteous and unselfish today. Give her a good night's rest tonight, and station angels all about her bed, for we ask it in Jesus' name. Amen."

Hugging her, the woman said, "I love you, Josie."

She felt a wet kiss on her cheek and then heard a little voice say, "I love you too, Miss Ellie, and I love Jesus, too."

Ellie wondered what Josie's attitude would be after spending an afternoon at home. What kind of environment would the girl be in on Christmas Day? She hoped the family would be considerate enough not to smoke in Josie's presence. The child didn't need any irritants or additional congestants in her lungs.

The week after Christmas, when Ellie came to the health-care center, Josie pulled her aside from the other children.

"Miss Ellie, I have something I want to give you." An impish grin indicated that she had something special to share. Taking the adult by the hand, the child walked to the bedstand next to her hospital bed and opened the drawer. "Close your eyes, Miss Ellie."

Dutifully she closed her eyes.

"Hold out your hand," Josie commanded.

Ellie sensed what felt to her to be a chain being placed in her hand.

"OK, Miss Ellie, now open your eyes."

When she did she found a ruby-red rosary lying in her palm. Being a Protestant, Ellie had always associated the rosary with ritualistic prayers. But as she looked at the smiling Josie standing in front of her, she realized that to this child the rosary represented something spiritual.

"My mommy gave it to me on Christmas Day, Miss Ellie, and I want you to have it."

"Why, Josie, I can't take your Christmas present!"

The girl's brow wrinkled. "I want *you* to have it." Her voice was firm and determined.

Ellie was having a difficult time correlating the rosary with what she knew of the behavior of Josie's mother. Perhaps it represented a step in the right direction for the woman, perhaps it signaled the realization of the seriousness of her daughter's condition, or perhaps it was a twinge of conscience that prompted it. Ellie didn't know. But she did know that Josie had never prayed the prayers that are to be said on each bead of the rosary, and she doubted that the girl even knew exactly how to use a rosary. But to Josie it represented God. And to Ellie the gift of the rosary said, "I have accepted your God. You represent God to me, and I want to give Him a gift."

That was one of the last times she saw Josie. As the children say, Josie "went home to heaven." But Ellie knows, according to Scripture (1 Corinthians 15:22, 23), that the child sleeps quietly awaiting the resurrection day.

The rosary is now a cherished reminder to her of a little girl's commitment to Jesus. And Ellie realizes that without a disease called cystic fibrosis, she and Josie may never have met. And perhaps Josie would never have met Jesus, either.